THE PHILOSOPHICAL
PROPAEDEUTIC

G. W. F. HEGEL
THE PHILOSOPHICAL PROPAEDEUTIC

Translated by A. V. Miller

Editors
Michael George and Andrew Vincent

Basil Blackwell

© Basil Blackwell Ltd, 1986

First published 1986

Basil Blackwell Ltd
108 Cowley Road, Oxford OX4 1JF, UK

Basil Blackwell Inc.
432 Park Avenue South, Suite 1503,
New York, NY 10016, USA

All rights reserved. Except for the quotation of short passages for the purposes of criticism and review, no part of this publication may be reproduced, stored in a retrieval system or transmitted, in any form or by any means, electronic, mechanical, photocopying, recording or otherwise, without the prior permission of the publisher.

Except in the United States of America, this book is sold subject to the condition that it shall not, by way of trade or otherwise, be lent, re-sold, hired out, or otherwise circulated without the publisher's prior consent in any form of binding or cover other than that in which it is published and without a similar condition including this condition being imposed on the subsequent purchaser.

British Library Cataloguing in Publication Data
Hegel, Georg Wilhelm Friedrich
　The philosophical propaedeutic.
　I. Title II. George, Michael
　III. Vincent, Andrew IV. Philosophische
Propädeutik. *English*
193　　　B2931
　ISBN 0–631–15013–7

Library of Congress Cataloging in Publication Data
Hegel, Georg Wilhelm Friedrich, 1770–1831.
　The philosophical propaedeutic Hegel.
　Translation of: Philosophische propädeutik.
　Bibliography: p.
　Includes index.
1. Philosophy–Introductions. I. George, Michael.
II. Vincent, Andrew. III. Title.
B2931.E5M54 1986   193   86–1033
ISBN 0–631–15013–7

Typeset by Oxford Publishing Services, Oxford
Printed in Great Britain by Page Bros (Norwich) Ltd

CONTENTS

Preface	vii
Acknowledgements	ix
Introduction	xi
Hegel's mature system in outline (1830)	xxxi
The parts of the *Propaedeutic* in relation to the 1830 system	xxxiii
The parts of the *Propaedeutic* in relation to the later works	xxxiv
1 The Science of Laws, Morals and Religion [For the Lower Class] *Rechts, Pflicht und Religionslehre für die Unterklasse* (1810)	1
2 Phenomenology [For the Middle Class] *Bewusssteinslehre für die Mittelklasse* (1809)	55
3 Logic [For the Lower Class] *Logik für die Unterklasse* (1809–10)	65
Logic [For the Middle Class] *Logik für die Mittelklasse* (1810–11)	74
The Science of the Concept [For the Higher Class] *Begriffslehre für die Oberklasse* (1809)	105
4 The Philosophical Encyclopaedia [For the Higher Class] *Philosophische Encyclopaedia für die Oberklasse* (1808)	124
Bibliography	170
Index	173

PREFACE

The translation has made reference to, and embodies in part, the translation of the *Propaedeutic* by W. T. Harris in the *Journal of Speculative Philosophy* during the 1860s. Reference has also been made to a manuscript translation undertaken by the English idealist thinker Thomas Hill Green whilst incumbent at Balliol College, Oxford during the 1850s and early 1860s. This manuscript is housed amongst the T. H. Green papers in Balliol College library. Its true identity came to light only in 1982 when, at the centenary conference on T. H. Green at Balliol, Michael George and Andrew Vincent recognized it amongst some of Green's papers on display in the library. Neither W. T. Harris nor T. H. Green made a complete translation of the text. Harris completed approximately two-thirds and Green approximately three-quarters of the Rosenkranz volume of the *Propaedeutic* in Hegel's *Werke*. A. V. Miller has completed the translation, has added sections since published in the Suhrkamp Verlag edition of Hegel's works and has fully revised the Harris translation utilizing the Rosenkranz, Hoffmeister and Suhrkamp texts. The work is therefore presented in a substantively new form. It has been ordered in the interest of preserving Hegel's pedagogical intentions rather than chronologically. It is the editors' intention to make of the text an introductory book for students of Hegel.

Bold type has been used for for the purpose of indicating those concepts which are central to Hegel's exposition and which he wishes to define: German equivalent terms are added in square brackets and in italics where the usual, or only available, English word employed in the translation is not deemed to fully or adequately render the meaning Hegel intended. The German practice of capitalizing the first letter of each noun has been retained for concepts which are central to Hegel's philosophy as a whole. Other concepts have been capitalized in those sections which are definitive of them. Words in italics reflect the emphasis to be found in the various German editions of Hegel's text. The translator and editors have not, however, felt themselves restricted in such emphasis by the German texts and have added their own emphasis where this was deemed appropriate. Certain sections have been amended in the manner of printing so as to list points which appear in the manuscript as continuous text. It is hoped that these practices will help the student new to Hegel to grasp more clearly that the work is primarily an exercise in concept definition at successively higher levels of development. Square brackets indicate a translator's addition and round brackets enclose Hegel's own explanatory comments.

It should also be remembered that the text of the *Propaedeutic* was never revised for publication by Hegel and therefore contains many incomplete sentences and *aides-mémoire* which Hegel included in order presumably to form a basis for extemporization in class. It should also be noted that some of the sections of the work, particularly those intended by Hegel for instruction in the lower class, may appear simple to the point of being uninformative. Such a view, however, is dangerous precisely because of the intricate web of concepts Hegel is trying to construct.

Michael George
Andrew Vincent

ACKNOWLEDGEMENTS

The editors wish to thank Suhrkamp Verlag, Frankfurt-am-Main, West Germany for their kind permission to translate hitherto unpublished sections of the *Propaedeutic* from their 1970 reprint of Hegel's works in *Werke* vol. 4, *Nürnberger und Heidelberger Schriften 1808–1817*. They would also like to thank the editors of *Educational Theory* for their kind permission to use in the introduction to this work parts of an article first published as 'Development and self identity: Hegel's concept of education' (A. W. Vincent and Michael George, *Educational Theory*, vol. 32 nos 3 and 4, pp. 131–41, Summer/Fall 1982).

The editors would also like to acknowledge the work of W. T. Harris, whose partial translation of the *Propaedeutic* was published in the *Journal of Speculative Philosophy* in the 1860s. Though extensively modified it nevertheless forms the basis of the first sections of the present translation. Also the editors wish to thank the Library of Balliol College, Oxford for their cooperation and kindness in making available to us the manuscript of an unpublished, partial translation of the *Propaedeutic* undertaken by T. H. Green around 1860. No part of Green's translation has been utilized in the present work.

INTRODUCTION

The manuscript of the *Philosophische Propaedeutic* was discovered in the autumn of 1838 by Karl Rosenkranz. Rosenkranz, Hegel's biographer, was at the time editing the collected edition of Hegel's works. The *Propaedeutic* turned up amongst some stray papers he was consulting. It was a very patchy text filled with Hegel's emendations and rewritings. Rosenkranz ordered the various paragraphs according to his own understanding of Hegel's purpose and published it as a separate volume (volume XVIII) of the collected works of 1840. Inevitably, Rosenkranz was selective in his structuring of the text. His ordering of the various sections presumably reflected his knowledge of Hegel's mature system and his acquaintance with Hegel's letters, specifically those to Niethammer, the head of the Protestant education department in Bavaria. Hoffmeister, who took over editorship of the Felix Meiner edition of Hegel's works from Georg Lasson, slightly restructured the sections of the *Propaedeutic* and added more material from Hegel's papers. In the 1970s Suhrkamp Verlag brought out a new edition, this time publishing the text of the *Propaedeutic* in a chronological order with further added material. The editors of the Suhrkamp edition completely abandoned the substantive curriculum ordering of the Rosenkranz text, moving as it does from the lower classes of the school to the higher classes, and instead structured the text on the chronological basis of the years in which Hegel wrote each particular section. This chronological ordering, though giving the text a more scholarly veneer, does not really contribute in any way to its comprehension. In fact it positively hinders it. It is certainly the case that Hegel left no definitive instructions as to the form in which he wished the whole to be read. The form of the whole is therefore open, the content being a compilation of Hegel's own writings, notes, jottings and fair student copies. Rosenkranz was solely responsible for making a book out of the various writings at his disposal. It is unlikely that Rosenkranz substantively altered the text, apart from making a few minor corrections, because Rosenkranz was a close friend of both Hegel and of his widow and was entrusted by the family with the task of aiding the publication of Hegel's collected works in the 1830s. What Rosenkranz did however was to try, as an editor must, to clarify, simplify and unify the diverse material before him. If there is therefore any criticism to be made about the manner in which Rosenkranz undertook his task it must be based upon a sympathetic assessment of his over zealous determination to make Hegel available to the readers of his day.[1]

Hegel structured the *Propaedeutic* in order to fit it into the various years of the school curriculum. One reason why it is now so difficult to order the sections is that Hegel constantly changed his mind as to the best means of introducing his pupils to philosophy. Initially, under pressure from Niethammer, Hegel had begun with the Logic, as he was later to do in his *Philosophical Encyclopaedia*. However, around 1812 he seems to have altered his views somewhat. The introductory course began now with what he saw as the more practical subjects; social, legal, moral and religious studies. The final year in which he taught his Encyclopaedia was used as a résumé of the whole system, although Hegel also included some material on aesthetics for fourth-year students. The present editors have therefore been faced with a problem of how best to present the *Propaedeutic* as a book. It is hoped that in seeking to make an introductory text out of the whole the editors are in accord with Hegel's own spirit and intentions. The purpose of making this work available to English readers is to enable them to have access to Hegel's system of philosophy, in its various parts, without immersing themselves immediately in the fuller, more complex writings. The editors have therefore adopted an ordering which reflects, as best as they are able, the mature system in microcosm. For this reason the parts have been ordered according to subject headings, subdivided by reference to the class levels in which each section was delivered. The first year was for the lower class (*Unterklasse*) with an age range of 14–15 years; the second year was for the middle class (*Mittelklasse*) with an age range of 15–18 years; and the third year was for the higher class (*Oberklasse*) with an age range of 17–20 years. By structuring the text upon these principles it is hoped to make it possible for readers unacquainted with Hegel to begin each section at the most elementary level and to advance gradually from there to the fuller exposition.

Introduction

HEGEL'S EDUCATIONAL THEORY

The *Propaedeutic* was written between 1808 and 1811, whilst Hegel was Rector at the Nuremberg Gymnasium. He had already had several years experience of teaching at various levels. From 1795 to 1801 he had acted as a private tutor for the children of the Steiggers von Tschugg family in Berne and the Gogels in Frankfurt. He left Frankfurt for Jena in 1801 to take up the post of privat-docent at the University. While at Jena he completed his first major work, the *Phenomenology of Spirit*. The stay in Jena came to an abrupt end in 1807 with the entry of Napoleon's army into the city. Hegel was for a year thereafter employed as the editor of a Catholic newspaper, the *Bamberger Zeitung*, a position he quite obviously enjoyed. However, he sought greater job security, and in 1808 Niethammer found him the post of Rector and Professor of Philosophy at the Gymnasium, or classical school for boys, at Nuremberg. Niethammer was keen to introduce elementary courses in philosophy and religion to school children, an enthusiasm not shared whole-heartedly by Hegel. Whilst at Nuremberg Hegel wrote one of the richest works of his life the *Science of Logic*, the so-called larger *Logic*, published in 1816. This work and the *Phenomenology* brought sufficient academic standing for him to be offered three chairs in philosophy; at Berlin, Heidelberg and Erlangen. Owing to the uncertainty about the Berlin offer Hegel accepted the chair at Heidelberg. However, he moved to Berlin in 1818 where he continued to write and pursue his philosophical interests until his death in 1831.

It is necessary to correct the popular image of Hegel as a 'heavy Germanic university philosopher'. Hegel was thirty-eight years old when appointed to the Nuremberg post. He was forty-five when he acquired his first full-time salaried academic post at the University of Heidelberg. If we include the periods of his private tutorships, Hegel had spent approximately fourteen years, quite successfully it appears, as a house and school teacher instructing children and young adults between the ages of fourteen and nineteen. This neither dampened his philosophical interest nor restricted his writing. Many of these years of teaching, specifically in the Gymnasium, were spent instructing the fourteen- to twenty-year-old age groups in philosophy. The *Propaedeutic* formed the basis of this instruction.

Each class at the Gymnasium entailed teaching for approximately four hours per week. Since all the years were taught concurrently, the total was some twelve hours per week. Hegel prepared his lessons utilizing fairly short paragraphs for each section which he would read aloud and then explain at greater length during the remaining period. The structure of each lesson was standard and required pupils to recapitulate, systematically, what had been learned from the previous week's lesson. Hegel encouraged questions and discussion of the topic, sometimes, it appears, spending the whole hour covering difficulties, of which no doubt there were many. He then dictated notes from the text of the *Propaedeutic*, which notes he expected to be supplemented later by the written homework in which he was such a great believer.

In and out of class Hegel was noted as a disciplinarian. He believed in obedience by the child, though there is no suggestion of physical punishment being used. Lessons quite often involved learning by rote before discussion. Hegel had a definite philosophical reason for this. The individual mind must have something to work with. It cannot think in a void. Originality and uniqueness in thought do not arise from an intellectual vacuum. Inventiveness derives from the assimilation of the substance of thought. Hegel saw his function as a teacher as 'dinning' the substance of thought into the pupils so that the foundations of thought processes could be laid.

The purpose of the *Propaedeutic* is threefold and can be fairly simply stated. Primarily it was designed as an elementary introduction to the study of philosophy, specifically for those going on to university study. It hardly needs to be said that Hegel's idea of the scope and nature of philosophy is different from today's. Secondly, and more importantly, it provided an overall pattern and structure to the school curriculum. Hegel thought that his system embodied the principles of the various disciplines in the school curriculum. The children would see the overall point of studying the various subjects and could apprehend the interconnections between them. The final aim of the actual teaching of the *Propaedeutic* was moral instruction, although this point has to be carefully examined.

The latter two points, which elucidate the general intentions of the *Propaedeutic*, require expansion. On the question of the school curriculum it must be noted that Hegel thought of his philosophy as encapsulating the essence of reality. The system, overall, shows the human mind trying to apprehend itself through its history and in and through the natural world of which it is so much a part. Politics, morality, religion, history, the natural sciences and so forth provide manifold illustrations of this theme. The pupils in studying the various subjects would be able to see their work in a more systematic perspective. We must remember that in Hegel's time it was still possible to claim an encyclopaedic mentality. As one Hegel scholar has put it: 'It was still possible to read, and to have read, all the masterpieces of the Greeks and Romans, and of European literature and philosophy, and to try at the same time to keep up with the sciences. Hegel's philosophy confronts us as the work of a man who has not shunned this tremendous effort.'[2] In tracing the movement of thought by which the world is developing, Hegel believed that he was uncovering the process by which the individual unfolds what is within himself. The purpose of the philosophical sciences is the same as education, namely making Mind known to itself or making itself its own object. The educated individual is one who has assimilated the world conceptually and realizes his identity with Mind (Spirit). Such an individual is 'at home in the world'. The particular individual must, necessarily, pass through the preformed stages of Spirit. He must traverse in microcosm, as it were, the macrocosm of human history and the knowledge which humanity has accrued to itself. This is the precondition both of the development of Spirit itself and of the individual. It becomes 'transparent' as it is recapitulated in the understanding of each new generation. This is therefore the essence of the educational process embodied, in embryo, in the *Propaedeutic*, and in maturity, in the *Encyclopaedia*.

The content of education in respect of the school curriculum is to be derived from the formative stages of Spirit. The various structural stages through which Spirit has passed in history provides the factual or material element which it is the purpose of the curriculum to communicate to the child. Hegel puts it so in his *Phenomenology of Spirit*: 'Thus as far as factual information is concerned, we find that what in former ages engaged the attention of men of mature minds, has been reduced to the level of facts, exercises and even games for children; and, in the child's progress through the school, we shall recognize the history of the cultural development of the world traced, as it were, in a silhouette.'[3] The acquisition of this knowledge is not merely a process of passive absorption, though learning by rote has a definite place; it also entails an active 'entering into' the very process by which Spirit has attained its self-realization. In his second Nuremberg *School Address* Hegel says that 'if learning limited itself to mere receiving, the effect would not be much better than if we wrote sentences on water: for it is not the receiving but the self-activity of comprehension and the power to use it again, that first makes knowledge our possession'.[4] The *Propaedeutic* represents Hegel's attempt to make his system, based upon the formative stages of Spirit, the basis of the school curriculum. It was designed to introduce the child in an active way to the acquisition of the previously accumulated totality of human knowledge, what Hegel terms 'Spirit'.

Hegel did, at times, speculate that the classics ought to be accorded a more prominent place than philosophy in the Gymnasium's curriculum. The reason for this was that the classics of Greece and Rome allow the child, in Hegel's view, to 'distance himself' from his own immediate interests and particular historical situation. This is something that philosophy does more abstractly. The virtue of the classics resides, therefore, in the fact that they are, for the child, an alien world and one to which he can readily relate unencumbered by any prejudices derived from his own situation. Yet they provide him with a means to acquire the basic structures of thought which, at a later stage, will become the foundation of his understanding and appreciation of his own present world. Of the ancient writings Hegel says: 'The perfection and grandeur of these masterpieces must be the intellectual bath, the secular baptism, which gives the mind its first and indelible tone and tincture in respect of good taste and knowledge.'[5] As Gadamer comments on this theme, in Hegel 'we recognize the classicists' prejudice that it is particularly the world of classical antiquity in which the universal nature of Spirit can be most easily found. To seek one's own in the alien, to become at home in it, is the most basic movement of Spirit, whose being is a return to itself from what is other.'[6] In order that the child may derive the fullest benefit from these writings, it is necessary that he becomes familiar with the essence of the Greek world. The child must be taught to appreciate the ancient cultures from an internal perspective. Such a perspective is only to be attained through a comprehension of the classical languages themselves. The child must not study these classical writings and authors without first having become proficient in the languages in which they were originally written. Their study provides the child with the capacity to understand the 'grammar' of Greek thought, and through a thorough grounding in the nature of the language he becomes aware of the depth and profundity of the Greek world. When the child has learnt to appreciate the relationship between language and consciousness of the world which it expresses, then he has taken the first step towards the understanding of his own language and age. Hegel, interestingly, saw little value in translations, as he says: 'Translations give us, to some extent the meaning, but not the form, not in its inner ethereal soul. They are like artificial roses which may resemble nature in shape, colour, perhaps even in smell, but the charm, tenderness and delicacy of life is not theirs. Language is the musical element, the element of intimacy which disappears in translation, the fine fragrance by means of which the soul's sympathy may be enjoyed but without which a classic work tastes like Rhine wine that has lost its flavour.'[7] One suspects this was a peculiarly meaningful analogy for Hegel.

Apart from the value of the classics in providing a source of ideas, in helping to develop the moral sensitivities of the child, and in awakening his mind to beauty, they also possess a functional value as a prerequisite to university study. This however is of secondary significance, their primary importance being to establish the preconditions necessary for the development of the child's capacity for participation in the life of his society as a full citizen. The classics emphasized the duties of the citizen. This theme was strengthened in the school curriculum by military exercises. Just as the Greeks had been prepared to defend their nation, civilization and culture when it was threatened by external enemies, so ought the modern citizen to be taught the means by which to defend his own society and state. In the Greek polis the obligation to military service was correlative with the enjoyment of citizenship. Military service, and the willingness to risk one's life for the state, served to strengthen the individual's identification with the political structures and the life of his state. In the modern world, however, the obligation to contribute towards the defence of society had, for Hegel, been greatly diminished by the creation of standing armies.

In placing the primary emphasis upon the classics as a means of education in schools, Hegel did not mean to devalue the study of the natural sciences and mathematics. These subjects, however, were of secondary importance, for their content did not lend itself to the communication of ideas, or to the instilling of ethical concepts. The natural sciences and mathematics are the means by which man may attain to the ends which he has set himself, but they play no part for Hegel in the determination of those ends. This is the prerogative of the liberal sciences, of which, so far as the education of the young is concerned, classics is accredited a place of high eminence if not quite one of pre-eminence.

Hegel's interest in the classics still did not stop him speculating on the precise role of the teacher, specifically in the teaching of philosophy on the curriculum. His general unease is reflected in his letters to Niethammer. Two letters of 23 October 1812 provide a fairly detailed review of his thought.[8] Hegel confessed that his thoughts were incomplete and that he was not settled in his own mind as regards the nature of philosophical instruction. He raised the issue that the study of the classics might be better adapted to the needs of the Gymnasial youth – although he confessed, with tongue in cheek, that he should not lay too much stress on this otherwise he would be putting himself out of a job. His remarks on the introductory classes in philosophy are divided into two parts, firstly, those concerned with the topics taught, and secondly, those on the methods of teaching.

The programme that Hegel here outlines is very similar to the general structure adopted by Rosenkranz in his first edition of the *Propaedeutic*, although the second year includes Cosmology and Natural Theology. Logic is reserved for the intermediate class with Psychology. Psychology, in the Rosenkranz edition, is dealt with in the section on Phenomenology. Hegel had in fact dealt with the topic of Psychology in his *Phenomenology of Spirit*. Yet in his later *Encyclopaedia of the Philosophical Sciences*, Part Three, the Philosophy of Mind, Psychology was a late addition to the section on Subjective Mind. It is dealt with as a dialectical mediation of Anthropology and Phenomenology. It is an odd addition even in the mature system since it repeats and overlaps much of the Phenomenology section.

Hegel maintained that the subjects of Religion, Law and Ethics contain material which is more directly practical and consequently easier for the children to grasp. The concepts within Law and Morality are more immediate and definite for the child. Logical forms are only shadows of the real and therefore harder to grasp. The second stage of the course would include logical, psychological and metaphysical ideas. Hegel contended that logic is simpler than psychology, since the former deals with abstractions whereas the latter deals with the highly complex and concrete. He divided Psychology into two parts: (a) Phenomenal Mind or Spirit; (b) Spirit in-and-for-itself. The first part deals, as it does in the mature Encyclopaedia, with the phases covered in the Phenomenology, namely, Consciousness, Self-Consciousness and Reason. In the second part, Feeling, Conception and Imagination are discussed. Within the discussion on Logic, Hegel believed that the Kantian Antinomies and Natural Theology should be discussed in dialectical terms. The Antinomies introduce the arguments for the existence of God and can be dialectically criticized, thereby leading to Hegel's own perspective on logic.

The final year was to be a review of the General Encyclopaedia, embracing the entire content of philosophy; the main subdivisions were Logic, the Philosophy of Nature and the Philosophy of Spirit. Conscious of the fact that he had covered much of the material in previous years, Hegel maintained that his treatment would only be cursory. He also admitted that there would be some problems in dealing with the Philosophy of Nature, partly because many of the children regarded it as boring and irrelevant. The Mind also had to 'grasp what is opposed to the Concept, into the Concept'; in other words, it had to transform natural objects and processes into conceptual form. Children lack both the intellectual vigour and the knowledge to pursue such an enterprise successfully. Thus each subject in the Encyclopaedia would be taught within the various years of the Gymnasium. The only subjects which would not be accorded detailed treatment were the Philosophy of Nature, the Philosophy of History and Aesthetics.

Hegel went on in the letter of October 1812 to review the methods of teaching. It is common, Hegel maintained, to think that one can separate philosophical thought from the content about which one philosophizes. Hegel believed that the two cannot be separated so easily. It is in reviewing the content that one learns to philosophize. It is through the careful, systematic study of the content of law, morality, religion and suchlike that one learns the highest thoughts in philosophy. Philosophy is a systematic complex of 'Sciences' full of content. Absolute knowledge is possible through a grasp of the totality of all the sciences. Philosophy devoid of both a content and systematic structure is haphazard, empty and fragmentary. Grasping the content of the sciences is grasping the essence of philosophy. To think through detailed material in class and in homework is to re-enact the principle of thought itself. The mathematical problem and its solution, the proof about the existence of God and its critique, the theory about the nature of light, all, when thought through, become part of my thought process. A teacher must possess the knowledge himself and think it through in front of the children. The pupil must then take on the hard 'labour of the Notion', i.e. think though the problem himself and 'possess' it.

In this process of teaching, content is given to the pupil's minds, which content replaces mere opinion. The school is not a place for the advancement of knowledge, rather it is concerned with the filling of empty heads with the rich existing body of thought. It overcomes the child's natural tendency to caprice. Hegel, quite obviously, has little time here for the Rousseauist ideals of education as expressed in *Émile*. The aim overall in philosophy is therefore to 'get the thought of the universe into the heads of the children'.

We will conclude this section with some remarks on moral instruction in the school. Hegel is not interested primarily in giving the pupils direct instruction; rather he thinks that morality will be inculcated gradually through the systematic study of the various subjects comprising the curriculum, most specifically the liberal sciences, with the classics and philosophy being accredited key roles. What is here being suggested by Hegel is an indirect form of intellectual socialization. However, as emphasized earlier, this is not simply a passive receptivity but rather involves the critical self-activity of the pupil's mind assimilating the knowledge. This whole process may be described as an intellectual 'Bildung'.

The idea of Bildung originated with the poet C. M. Wieland and gained considerable popularity with the *Bildungsroman* tradition in eighteenth-century German literature, reaching its zenith in Goethe's *Wilhelm Meisters Lehrjahre* and Schiller's *Wilhelm Tell*. This tradition was concerned to trace out, in detail, the total, harmonious development of an individual through a diverse range of social and moral experiences. Bildung is the process of such a development. The development of the child from a natural and instinctive will to a rational willing is the Bildung of that individual child. Hegel employs the idea to explain the development of Mind or Spirit in the individual, in cultures and in world history. It also explains the intellectual and moral development of the child through the school curriculum. The pupil is forced to sacrifice his immediate interests or idiosyncrasies to the experience of the systematic demands of thought, as embodied in the curriculum. Each subject or science, each form of consciousness, must be thought through, assimilated and ultimately transcended as something external and made something *for me* as *this* educated and socialized individual. For Hegel this is the process of the gradual development of freedom within each man, within his society and state and finally within his history. As Hegel puts it 'the final purpose of education . . . is liberation and the struggle for higher liberation still; education is the absolute transition from an ethical substantiality which is immediate and natural to one which is intellectual and so both infinitely subjective and lofty enough to have attained universality of form.'[9] Education and thus Bildung are regarded as an intellectual advance. They begin with the child at the level of instinct. Freedom is here simply following out immediate desires without obstruction. The guidance of the child towards intellectual concerns is described by Hegel as a 'second birth'.[10] The individual in the school is no longer identified by his idiosyncrasies. The single, individual, consciousness is an empty husk. Individuality is not uniqueness. Individuality is manifest in the 'Bildung of Spirit'. As Hegel put it: 'This reshaping of the soul, this alone is what education means. The more educated a man is, the less is there apparent in his behaviour anything peculiar only to him, anything that is merely contingent.'[11] Freedom or liberation is an active internalization of the universal (as manifest in the existing body of knowledge) into the subjective will of the individual. Rational thought becomes habitual and overcomes all capriciousness. The result, for Hegel, is the ethical citizen.

The *Propaedeutic*, as the foundation of the school curriculum, ensures therefore the 'mediation' of human character and will – its absorption into the wider social ethos of which it is itself a constituent part. Education of course does not begin here. In the family, for example, much of the normative or ethical content is unconsciously assimilated via love, trust and natural feeling. In the school norms are more systematically and theoretically inculcated. This process is continued to a much higher level in the university. Finally, in civil society, after formal schooling is completed, the individual comes to recognize his dependence on his fellow citizens and to share in the pursuit of his common interests via the state. Thus the educational process of Bildung goes on in society itself. Education generally, by retracing the path of Spirit's self-realization, raises the individual's subjectivity to a recognition of the rationality underpinning the social institutions of *his* society. The individual who has undergone this process of education has had his subjectivity brought into conformity with the historical progress of mankind as manifested in the social institutions, customs and ethical precepts of his age. By thinking through the history of 'Thought' and the ideals of humanity, the pupils slowly assimilate the content of morality into their thought processes. The *Propaedeutic* therefore, encapsulates for Hegel the form and content of the course of instruction necessary, so he believed, to bring the child of the modern world into that state of intellectual appreciation which alone would enable him to participate as an active, rational, informed, and concerned citizen of his society and age.

The *Propaedeutic* and the System of Philosophy

The *Philosophical Propaedeutic* is of significance for a number of reasons. With perhaps the exception of parts of the Jena lectures it may be said that this work is Hegel's only real attempt to encompass the totality of his philosophy within one text. Admittedly the detailed ordering of the text is not always that of the mature writings and some of the categories only briefly broached here by Hegel undergo considerable further development in the *Encyclopaedia*. None the less the basic ideas and structure of the mature system is here in microcosm.

If the present student of this translation first reads The Philosophical Encyclopaedia [For the Higher Class] he will encounter, in this shortened version of the system, the greater part of Hegel's ideas and concepts. Though the text cannot be said to make Hegel easy as an introduction, it presents the beginning student of Hegel with far less sheer verbiage than is found in the later writings. As such it is the editors' hope that this book will enable those unfamiliar with Hegel's system to begin to plumb the depth therein. However it is recommended that this work be read not in isolation but rather as a guide for a wider study in which reference is made to other authorities on Hegel and to the full Hegelian system in the mature works. Whilst it has not proven possible to provide a detailed commentary for the text, this general introduction has been added with a view to providing a degree of elucidation in respect of the more complex parts of the work.

The *Propaedeutic* may be divided into three principal parts: The Logic, Moral and Social Philosophy, and The Encyclopaedia. Of these the first and the third are the most closely linked. As in the later works, the Encyclopaedia contains the Philosophy of Nature which, as the objectification of the Idea or Spirit, represents the concrete expression of Hegel's philosophy rather than the purely conceptual formulation of it in the Logic itself. The Philosophy of Mind may be said to encompass the elementary Phenomenology of Spirit and the Moral and Social Philosophy. The Moral and Social Philosophy is also used as an introductory element for the lower class. What follows is therefore a brief summary based upon this classification and as such may be read as applying also to the mature formulation of Hegel's philosophy.

Logic

The Logic is concerned with the form of thought, with pure thought considered as founded upon concepts which are at once individual and interconnected one with another. It is the realm of 'abstract thought', namely that realm which is based upon the capacity for language, for abstraction and abstract reasoning and upon what Hegel terms the Concept or Notion. It is also pre-eminently the realm of dialectical reasoning. It is not a work in the modern sense of the word 'logic'; nor is its foundation even that of Aristotle and the syllogistic style that Hegel was familiar with. The dialectical logic of Hegel is founded upon a sense of necessity quite distinct from any formal logical system. It is perhaps best understood as a necessary interconnection and dependency of concepts one upon another. For example, the first triadic movement in the Logic, that of Being, Nothing, Becoming, is characteristic of the whole system of thought. This triad is explained in some detail below.

Nature

Whereas in the logic Hegel is dealing with ideas or thought, in the philosophy of nature he is examining what is apparently an external existence. As he states repeatedly – thought provides universal abstract categories, but the content or substance of representations or perceptions is taken from experience of something apparently external. In this sense nature appears as 'outside' thought. Hegel refers to it as 'other-being' or spirit as other. The existent Idea is nature. The philosophy of nature therefore deals with the varieties of existence which correspond to our ideas. Nature or the natural world is the cradle out of which human consciousness and spirit develop. It is thus, for Hegel, an essential preliminary to any account of human consciousness or social development. Yet the apparent external aspect of nature is viewed by Hegel as a stage in the development of human consciousness. In the philosophy of nature the human mind treats nature as an external object. After a detailed review of notions of matter, motion, space and time, and the development of organic life in plants and animals, the philosophy of nature arrives at consciousness. Hegel's review of these stages is based on the sciences of his own time. Such sciences are reliant on the notion of externality. Yet in the moment of consciousness mind or spirit realizes that *it* had created or presupposed the separate existence of nature. Nature ultimately has no existence independent from mind. Its apparent externality is really a phase in the development of the human mind. Therefore there is nothing intrinsically wrong for Hegel with a theory of an external world as long as one realizes that such a theory is mind-dependent.

Spirit [Mind]

This is for Hegel the most central term in his philosophy. The German word *Geist* which Hegel employs can be translated with equal validity as Mind or Spirit. The tendency has been for Right Hegelians to employ the latter term in order to give to Hegel's philosophy a religious tone and to emphasize its supposed compatibility with Christianity. On the other hand, Left Hegelians have tended to see *Geist* in terms of Mind and thus as quintessentially anthropomorphic and pantheistic in its implications. The political dimension of the translation aside, the term is of considerable importance in Hegel's philosophy because it represents the active principle behind the whole of creation. As such it is a 'subject' as opposed to a lifeless 'substance' *qua* Spinoza and it renders the whole of Hegel's system of philosophy as essentially dynamic rather than ontologically static. It is *Geist* which *realizes* or *actualizes* itself variously in man, in human society and in history. It permeates not only the natural world, but also the world of man or Subjective Spirit. Spirit presents itself in the world as a dichotomy between Nature and Man, between the objective and the subjective elements in perception and thus of course in the epistemological problem of how man 'comes to know the world'. The dichotomy between subject and object is also the basis of man's sense of 'alienation', the sense of not 'being at home in the world', which is the human condition and which mankind has sought to heal via philosophical enquiry for more than two thousand years. Hegel's system of philosophy, as the exposition in rational terms of the progress of *Geist*, is the 'intellectual' means of healing this sense of estrangement from the world. Because both the human mind and the objective world are the product of one and the same process, in *Geist* it is possible for the subject, man, to have knowledge of the objective, the physical world. This knowledge is of two kinds: firstly, the sum total of the logical 'Concepts' which describe the world; and secondly, the 'logical' means by which these Concepts interconnect one with another and are mutually related and dependent. This is the purpose of the Logic in Hegel's philosophy. It provides the bare skeletal outline of both the physical and human world. It should not, however, be thought of as a mere abstract representation of the world because for Hegel there can be no epistemological divide between the world and human understanding and knowledge. The schema of universal Concepts which mankind employs to understand the world are 'concrete universals' which are in the very stuff of the world and are there to be distilled from it. Mankind and the natural world partake of the same fundamental 'ground' and the same 'Reason' governs both. As such the Logic is the rational exposition of the underlying Reason of existence, a Reason which for Hegel is everywhere manifest and present.

Spirit is therefore best understood as the spiritual and mental active principle in Hegel's system which develops in the world in and through Reason, and as the creation of that reality which is 'understood' and explicated via the dialectic in the Logic and the whole *Encyclopaedia of the Philosophical Sciences*.

Some philosophical terms in the *Propaedeutic*

Being in-itself and for-itself

Actu and *potentia*: A Concept of a thing 'in-itself' is what it is in its potential, what it is as a mere intellectual understanding. What a thing is 'for-itself' is what in it has become realized or actualized, i.e. what in its Concept has developed from potentiality into reality. The whole of creation is the process of the development of Reason via Spirit to the complete explicit presentation of what is implicit and 'in-itself': i.e. a movement from the 'in-itself' to the 'for-itself'. This movement is complete when the thing is what it is 'in-and-for itself' and has become 'actual'. The famous phrase attributed to Hegel, 'what is real is rational and what is rational is real', is an expression of this idea. What has become 'real' or 'actual' is fully rational because it corresponds to a Concept or Notion (*Begriff*) and thus to Reason as such. Conversely only that which is rational, i.e. that which is contained in the Concept of a thing, can become actual or 'realized'.

Immediate and mediated relations

If I engage in social intercourse with someone I am in a state of 'immediate relation' for Hegel. If however I sell something to someone else I cannot be said then to stand in such an immediate relation; rather my relationship to another is 'mediated' because a Contract is something which not merely involves two parties but also entails law, the agencies of enforcement, etc. The formal duties which I have to another person in respect of a contract are determined not by myself but by the state. The two contracting parties may determine the 'content' of a contract, but that the contract is enforced, is drawn up in accordance with legal norms, is something which I undertake 'mediatedly' towards another. Any relation, logical, social, political, etc., which entails a reference to and a dependency upon something external to the immediate condition, is said to by Hegel to be 'mediated'.

Sublation, moment and the first dialectical triad

The German verb *aufheben* is central to Hegel's entire philosophical system because it is the operative term of the dialectic. In the Logic each concept or set of concepts is said to be 'sublated' at a higher stage of thought and conceptualization and this process is the dialectic at work. The German term has the dual and contradictory senses of 'abolition' and 'preservation'. Thus what is 'sublated' is at once negated but also reformulated at a different level. The proverbial little acorn which becomes the mighty oak tree may be said to have become negated by the oak which it becomes and yet to have been preserved in so far as the structure of the acorn is potentially what the oak has actually become. The process of development, in this case in the physical rather than the logical realm, is a series of 'moments' within one fluid, dynamic whole. The acorn is thus one moment of a process which ends with the oak, it itself being a moment of the whole process of its growth, existence and death.

On the logical level it is perhaps best to provide an example of what Hegel means by way of an elucidation of the first triadic relation in the Logic – a relation which has perplexed not only those new to the study of Hegel but some scholars who are very familiar indeed with his work.

The first logical transition is that of the moments of Being and Nothing and their sublation in the concept of Becoming.

Hegel claims that Being cannot be 'thought', for as a concept it has no qualities, no 'determinations', and thus is ungraspable as an idea. Following Kant, and rejecting Parmenides, Hegel finds no predicates at all in the concept of Being and denies that it is a predicate at all. On the contrary it is the condition of all predicates, the copula in the first part of any proposition of the kind 'This is'. Being then is the most common of all ideas, as it is the condition of and is shared by all existent entities. Yet we cannot, if we attempt to think what pure Being is 'in itself', arrive at a definite specific quality. Indeed we arrive at the opposite conclusion and are forced to accept that pure Being is the same as pure Nothing, for it is without any quality, quantity, differentiation, etc. If we now attempt to think what pure Nothing is and to arrive at a similar quality we are again frustrated. Yet in this instance our frustration is not unexpected, because Nothing is a concept for which we would not anticipate being able to find a definite quality. However, when we try to 'think' the concept Nothing as a concept we are forced to ascribe at least one determinate quality to it, that of the lack or absence of all qualities. Logically we are thus in a strange world. The concept of Being produces the definition 'a complete indeterminacy' or 'a lack of any content'. The result negates not only the endeavour but also what we have been logically expecting, for surely Being is something and as such should be definable in positive and not merely negative terms. Nothing as a concept, on the other hand, is also perplexing. We are obliged to try to 'think' Nothing, to derive some concept of it, and yet this is contrary to what we should logically expect. Even though our result produces a negative definition, namely the absence of all determinations, we have at least some definition for the idea, namely this very idea of the negation of all predicates. The two definitions for Being and Nothing are thus found to be the same and, as such, are the basis of the claim by Hegel that Being and Nothing are conceptually the same. Nevertheless, as Hegel well recognizes, it is not the same thing to say that something 'is' and 'is not'. We are forced to hold these concepts as distinct even if our logical enquiry seems to frustrate this. What Concept, asks Hegel, holds these ideas as distinct and whilst embracing them and being logically dependent upon them is nevertheless a Concept of which something definite can be said? The answer is the Concept of Becoming.

The verb *werden* in German cannot strictly be rendered in English by the word Becoming because firstly, unlike in English, it is the German means of forming the future tense, and secondly it is somewhat less precise in its connotation than the English term Becoming. In fact for Hegel the term *werden* means 'becoming' in the sense of 'coming-to-be' and also its opposite 'ceasing-to-be'. The idea of anything 'coming-to-be' or 'ceasing-to-be' requires two determinate states of affairs, the idea of Being as such and of Nothing, for what 'comes-to-be' comes out of nothing into being and what 'ceases-to-be' reverses the process. The concept of Becoming, as Hegel defines it, therefore is dependent upon the concepts of Being and Nothing and therefore preserves them, but also transcends them and negates the continuous passing back and forth between them in search of some difference which frustrated us at the previous level. The process is thus one of 'building' as it were 'levels' of concepts and producing thereby a mutually interconnecting system of categories of thought. Each concept has its inherent limitation or 'boundary', i.e. that which it cannot resolve, and from this 'internal' self-negation of any concept is generated both the need to go beyond it and the means of utilizing that concept at some higher stage of thought. The entire Logic is therefore not merely 'logical', in the sense of exemplifying some form of implicative order, but is also an exposition of the 'necessary' transitions in our logical categories which the perplexities of the world force upon us in our endeavour to describe it. Each successive concept should therefore be thought of as the next necessary step required if human knowledge is to have the intellectual tools to accomplish its task.

Determinate being

What has here been translated as Determinate Being is the German word *Dasein* and is the concept which follows Becoming in the Logic. It has been rendered in this translation by the admittedly inadequate term 'Determinate Being'. This is partly because the term has become the most common means amongst English translators of rendering *Dasein* into English, and in part because Hegel himself defines *Dasein* as 'determinate Being' or in the German *bestimmte Sein*. However, a note of caution ought to be added here. The English word 'determinate' is a strong one in a way that the German *bestimmte* is not. Hegel means by *Dasein* not a fixed, definite, definable Being or a Being which has become something discernably specific. Rather he wishes to convey the idea of a state of Being which has become something permanent, something which, in some manner or other as yet undefined', can be said to possess 'stability' or 'presence'. Hegel has yet to derive the concepts of Quality or Quantity and as such he is unable to say of Determinate Being that it possesses any particular Quality or Magnitude. The idea of 'Becoming' as a constant changing state of affairs, as the continual arising and passing away of things, must be a 'Becoming' which is located in something permanent. Were it not so then what has arisen would decay and pass back into nothingness and the process of 'Becoming' would have abolished itself. To have an idea of a constant alternation between arising and passing away it is necessary that that which arises arises into some condition which itself is not governed by this process but which is permanent by virtue of the fact that at any one moment something is arising as something else is passing away. The idea of the 'permanent' background behind 'Becoming' is what is meant by *Dasein*.

Human will, rational will and particular will

This first set of definitions forms the beginning of the Science the Laws, Morals and Religion. Hegel's terminology is his own but the ideas upon which he is working have been derived directly from Immanuel Kant and the theory of the will which he formulated in the essay *On Radical Evil*. This essay was later republished as the first part of Kant's critique of religion, *Religion within the Bounds of Mere Reason Alone*.

Kant recognized that the ethical theory which he had expounded in his previous works suffered from one major defect. The Will had been defined as a 'Will of Choice', what Kant termed *Willkür*. If the Will was to be located within the 'phenomenal' self and thus within the domain of cause and effect, it would require a miracle to raise any man to the level at which he could become morally responsible. Even if he were still free to recognize and assent to the 'categorical imperative', the Moral Law, he would not be free to act upon the universal maxims he had assented to as a rational being. Nothing, bar the intervention of a higher power, could possibly free his Will from the dominance of physical cause and effect relations. As such it was essential, if man were to have the possibility of becoming actually moral, to postulate a Will which was 'free' in so far as it was able to decide whether to be governed by the 'appetites' (Hume's 'passions') or by the Moral Law of reason. This elementary level of freedom – to be directed by a desire, to decide which desire to follow, or to renounce each and every desire in favour of a moral ought, places man and his Will, as Pope puts it in the *Essay on Man*, 'on this isthmus of a middle state, A being darkly wise, and rudely great: ... He hangs between, in doubt to act or rest, In doubt to deem himself a god, or beast; In doubt his mind or body to prefer.'

However, the implications of this early theory effectively denied the possibility of holding anyone responsible for evil or even immoral actions. If the individual raised himself to the moral realm he was bound to act morally, for the Moral Law itself alone would be his motivation and guide. The man who remained at the level of the 'Lower Appetites' was 'unfree' and could therefore only be blamed for not having developed, as yet, a sufficient strength of Will to advance to the realm of reason and prefer the faculty of the 'Higher Appetite'. In the essay *Radical Evil* Kant proposed the idea that even the rational man could be immoral. No longer directed by the 'Lower Appetites' he nevertheless might say, as Milton put it in *Paradise Lost*, 'Evil be thou my Good.' As a 'free' agent he has freely chosen to renounce the Moral Law and to adopt, as a rational act, its very opposite. Such for Kant is Evil as opposed to mere Bad. Hegel retains these concepts and terms the Moral Law the Universal Law and gives to it a significance which transcends even that with which Kant had imbued the idea. The Universal Law of Reason is, for Hegel, the 'real' Will of each individual, that Higher Will which it is his duty to 'actualize' in his social and personal life. He thus speaks of recalcitrant individuals being brought to a recognition of their true nature, their 'higher' purpose. It is the purpose of punishment to bring criminals to the recognition of their own inner failings as well as to redress the imbalance produced by the original evil deed.

Unlike Kant, however, Hegel does not remain at the level of mere 'abstract' morality and moral theorizing. He seeks to advance to a 'practical' morality which is founded in the active lives of ordinary citizens of a state. He thus goes on to expound his conception of *Sittlichkeit* or a 'situated' ethic, as social ethicality, as opposed to the mere formalism of Kant's categorical imperative. In this 'higher' form of moral thinking the formal element of Kant's imperative is embraced and at the same time transcended. Whereas Kant wished to make of ethics a rigid and pre-eminently rational science, Hegel goes on to discuss the idea of a moral 'disposition', or what it is to live a practical life in harmony with one's fellow man from an innate but not necessarily rationally articulated sense of morality.

The later parts of the Science of Laws, Morals and Religion are concerned to define the institutions of social life as actually existent and to demonstrate their place in a scheme as mutually dependent elements of one political, social and ethical educational process. Each element, be it the family, or one of the organs of the State, is part of what it is for a society to exist as a series of individuals in a social context. Each element performs its unique functions both in the creation of this order and in its preservation. And each element at once constitutes and also reflects the prevailing moral ethos of that society. It is of course Hegel's purpose throughout to demonstrate how what is 'given', i.e. what has been produced by man during his history, be it on the social, political or conceptual level, is the result of a hidden process of 'Reason' and the product of *Geist* working its purpose out in the realms of space, time and human affairs.

NOTES TO INTRODUCTION

1 G. W. F. Hegel, *Werke* volume 18, ed. K. Rosenkranz (Berlin: Duncker and Humblot, 1840).
2 W. Kaufmann, *Hegel: a Reinterpretation* (Anchor Books, Doubleday and Company, 1966), p. 44.
3 G. W. F. Hegel, *The Phenomenology of Spirit*, trans. A. V. Miller (Oxford: Oxford University Press, 1979), p. 16.
4 G. W. F. Hegel, 'Second School Address', in M. Mackenzie, *Hegel's Educational Theory and Practice* (London: Swan Sonneschein, 1909), p. 167.
5 Ibid., p. 159.
6 Hans-Georg Gadamer, *Truth and Method*, trans. W. Glen-Doepel (London: Sheed and Ward, 1975), p. 15.
7 G. W. F. Hegel, 'The First School Address', in Mackenzie, *Hegel's Educational Theory and Practice*, p. 162.
8 Hegel, *Werke*, volume 17, ed. Rosenkranz, pp. 333–48.
9 G. W. F. Hegel, *The Philosophy of Right*, trans. T. M. Knox (Oxford: Oxford University Press, 1971), p. 125.
10 Ibid, addition, p. 260.
11 G. W. F. Hegel, *The Philosophy of Mind*, trans. W. Wallace (Oxford: Clarendon Press, 1971), addition, p. 52.

HEGEL'S MATURE SYSTEM IN OUTLINE

LOGIC

Being
    Quality
    Quantity
    Measure

Essence
    Ground of Existence
    Appearance
    Actuality

Concept (Notion)
    Subjective Concept (Notion)
    The Object
    The Idea

NATURE

Mechanics
    Space and Time
    Matter and Motion (Finite Mechanics)
    Absolute Mechanics

Physics
    Physics of the Universal Individuality
    Physics of the Particular Individuality
    Physics of the Total Individuality

Organics
    Terrestrial Organism
    The Plant Nature
    The Animal Nature

SPIRIT [MIND]

Subjective Mind
    Anthropology (Soul)
    Phenomenology of Mind (Consciousness)
    Psychology

Objective Mind	Law
	Morality of Conscience
	Moral Life or Social Ethicality

Absolute Mind	Art
	Revealed Religion
	Philosophy

THE PARTS OF THE *PROPAEDEUTIC* IN RELATION TO THE LATER WORKS

THE SCIENCE OF LAWS, MORALS AND RELIGION

Introduction
Science of Law
Science of Duties or Morals

PhR, PhH, EPhS (Part Three; Introduction, Section 2)

Science of Religion

LPhR, EPhS (Part three; Section 3, Subsection B), PS

PHENOMENOLOGY

Consciousness in General
Self-Consciousness
Reason

PS, EPhS (Part Three; Introduction, Section 1 Subsections B and C)

LOGIC

Being
Essence
The Concept

PS, EPhS (Part One), SL

THE SCIENCE OF THE CONCEPT

Science of the Concept
Realization of the Concept
Science of the Idea

SL (final section), EPhS (Part One, Third Subdivision)

THE PARTS OF THE *PROPAEDEUTIC* IN RELATION TO THE 1830 SYSTEM

LOGIC

Logic [For the Lower Class]
Logic [For the Middle Class]
The Science of the Concept [For the Higher Class]
The Philosophical Encyclopaedia [For the Higher Class]: First Part

NATURE

The Philosophical Encyclopaedia [For the Higher Class]: Second Part

SPIRIT [MIND]

Subjective Mind	Phenomenology [For the Middle Class]
	The Philosophical Encyclopaedia [For the Higher Class]: Third Part, First Section
Objective Mind	The Science of Laws, Morals and Religion [For the Lower Class]: Introduction
	The Philosophical Encyclopaedia [For the Higher Class]: Third Part, Second Section,
Absolute Mind	The Philosophical Encyclopaedia [For the Higher Class]: Third Part, Third Section
	Phenomenology [For the Middle Class]: Third Stage
	The Science of Law, Morals and Religion [For the Lower Class]: Third Part

THE PHILOSOPHICAL ENCYCLOPAEDIA

Logic	SL, EPhS (Part One)
Science of Nature	EPhS (Part Two)
Science of Spirit	EPhS (Part Three), PhR, PS, LA, LPhR, PhH

ABBREVIATIONS

See bibliography for details of publication.

EPhS	*Encyclopaedia of the Philosophical Sciences*
LA	*Hegel's Aesthetics*
LPhR	*Lectures on the Philosophy of Religion*
PhH	*Lectures on the Philosophy of History*
PhR	*The Philosophy of Right*
PS	*The Phenomenology of Spirit*
SL	*The Science of Logic*

1
THE SCIENCE OF LAWS, MORALS AND RELIGION
[For the Lower Class]

INTRODUCTION

1

The object of this science is the **Human Will** in its relations as the **Particular Will** to the **Universal Will**: to the Will which is Lawful and Just or in accordance with Reason. As Will the Mind stands in a practical relation to itself. The *practical* way of acting [*Verhalten*], through which it brings determination into its determinateness or opposes other determinations of its own in the place of those already existing in it without its cooperation, is to be distinguished from its *theoretical* way of acting.

2

Consciousness, as such, is the relation of the Ego to an object; this object may be internal or external. Our Knowing contains objects, some of which we obtain a knowledge of through Sensuous Perception; others, however, have their origin in the Mind itself. The former, taken together, constitute the **Sensuous World**; the latter, the **Intelligible World**. Judicial [*rechtlichen* = legal], ethical and religious conceptions belong to the latter.

3

In the relation of the Ego and object to each other the Ego is (a) *passive*; in which case the object is regarded as the cause of the determinations in the Ego and the particular ideas [*Vorstellungen*] which the Ego has are attributed to the impression made upon it by the immediate objects before it. This is the **Theoretical Consciousness**. Whether it be in the form of *perception* or of *imagination* or of the thinking activity its content is always a given and extant something, a content having existence independent of the Ego.

On the contrary, (b) the Ego manifests itself as **Practical Consciousness** when its determinations are not mere 'ideas' and thoughts, but issue forth into external existence. In this process the Ego determines the given things or objects, so that the former is active and the latter are passive, i.e. the Ego is the cause of changes in the given objects.

4

Practical Ability [*Vermögen*] as such determines itself from within, i.e. through itself. The content of its determinations belongs to it and it recognizes that content for its own. These determinations, however, are at first only internal and, for this reason, separated from the external reality, but they are to become external and be realized. This is done through the [conscious] **Act**. By such an Act internal practical determinations receive externality: i.e. external Being. Conversely, this process may be regarded as the cancelling of an extant externality and the bringing of the same into harmony with the internal determination.

5

The internal determination of the Practical Consciousness is either **Impulse** [*Trieb*] or **Will Proper** [*eigentlicher Wille*]. Impulse is a natural self-determination which rests upon circumscribed feelings and has a limited finite end in view which it cannot transcend. In other words, it is the unfree, immediately determined, **Lower Appetite** [*niedere Begehrungsvermögen*] according to which man ranks as a creature of nature. Through **Reflection** he transcends Impulse and its limitations, and not only compares it with the means of its gratification but also compares these means one with another and the impulses one with another, and both of these with the object and end of his own existence. He then yields to the decision of Reflection and gratifies the Impulse or else represses it and renounces it.

6

The **Will Proper**, or the **Higher Appetite**, is (a) pure *indeterminateness* of the Ego, which as such has no limitation or a content which is immediately extant through nature but is indifferent towards any and every determinateness. (b) The Ego can, at the same time, pass over to a *determinateness* and make a choice of some one or other and then actualize it.

7

The **Abstract Freedom** of the Will consists in this very indeterminateness, or identity of the Ego with itself, wherein a determination occurs only in so far as the Ego makes it its own [assimilates it] or posits it within itself. And yet in this act it remains self-identical and retains the power to abstract again from each and every determination. There may be presented to the Will, *from without*, a great variety of incitements, motives and laws but man, in following the same, does this only in so far as the Will itself makes these its own determinations and resolves to actualize them. This, too, is the case with the determinations of the Lower Appetites, or with what proceeds from natural Impulses and Inclinations.

8

The Will has **Moral Responsibility** [*Schuld*] in so far as (a) its determination is made its own solely from its own self, or by its resolve: i.e. [in so far as] the Ego wills it, and (b) it is conscious of the determinations which are produced through its act as they lie in its resolve or are necessarily and immediately involved in its consequences.

9

A **Deed** [*Tat*] is, as such, the produced change and determination of a Being. To an **Act** [*Handlung*], however, belongs only what lay in the resolve or was in the consciousness [and] hence what the Will acknowledges as its own.

10

The free Will, as free, is moreover not limited to the determinateness and individuality through which one individual is distinguished from another but is Universal Will and the individual is, as regards his Pure Will, a Universal Being.

11

The Will can, in various ways, take up into itself external content, that is, a content which does not proceed from its own nature and make this content its own. In this the Will remains self-identical only in form. It is, namely, conscious of its power to abstract from each and every content and recover its pure form but it does not remain self-identical as regards its content and essence. In so far as it is such a Will it is really only the **Will-of-Choice** [*Willkür*] [or **Arbitrariness**].

12

But that the Will may be *truly* and absolutely free it is requisite that what it wills, or its content, be naught else than the Will itself: i.e. the pure self-determination, or the act that is in harmony with itself. It is requisite that it wills only in-itself and has itself for its object. The **Pure Will**, therefore, does not will some special content or other on account of its speciality but in order that the Will as such may in its deed *be free* and be freely actualized; in other words, that the Universal Will may be done.

The more precise determination and development of these universal maxims of the [rational] Will belong to the **Science of Laws, Morals and Religion**.

Elucidation of the Introduction

1

Objects are particular somethings through their *determinations* as sensuous objects, for example, through their shape, size, weight, colour, through the more or less firm combination of its parts, through the purpose for which they are used, etc. If one, in his conception of it, takes away the determinations of an object, this process is called **Abstraction**. There remains after the process a less determined object: i.e. an **Abstract Object**. If, however, I conceive of only *one* of these determinations, this is called an **Abstract Representation** [or **Abstract Idea**]. The object left in its completeness of determination is called a **Concrete Object**. When I abstract all the determinations I have left only the conception of the *absolutely* **Abstract Object**. When one says 'Thing', though he may mean something quite definite, he says only something quite indefinite since our thought reduces an actual something to this abstraction of mere 'Thing'.

Sensuous Perception is in part external, in part internal. Through *external* [Sensuous Perception] we perceive things which are outside us in time and space, things which we distinguish from ourselves. Through the *internal* Sensuous Perception we take note of the states and conditions which belong in part to our bodies and in part to our souls. One part of the Sensuous World contains such objects and their determinations, as, for example, colours, that is, objects that have a sensuous basis and have received a mental form. If I say, 'This table is black', I speak in the first place of this single concrete object but, secondly, the predicate 'black' which I affirm of it is a general [quality] which belongs not merely to this single object but to several objects. 'Black' is a simple idea. We cognize a real concrete object immediately. This act of immediate apprehension is called **Intuition**.

A general Abstract Idea is therefore a mediated Idea for the reason that I know it by means of another, i.e. by means of abstraction or the omission of other determinations which are found united in the Concrete Object. A Concrete Idea is said to be analysed when the determinations which are united in it as concrete are separated. The intelligible world receives its content from Spirit [i.e. from the activity of the Mind], and this content consists of pure universal Ideas such, for example, as Being, Nothing, Attribute, Essence, etc.

2

The first source of our knowledge is called **Experience**. To Experience belongs this important feature: that we *ourselves* have perceived it. A distinction must however, be drawn between **Perception** and **Experience**. Perception has for its object only a single something which is determined in one way this moment and in another way the next moment. If I repeat the Perception, and in the repeated perceptions take note of what remains the same and hold it fast, this operation is properly termed Experience. Experience contains, for the most part, laws: i.e. [just] such a connection of two phenomena that if one is extant, the other one must result from it in all cases. The Experience contains, however, only the mere *generality* of such a phenomenon and not the *necessity* of the connection. Experience teaches only that things are or happen thus and so but not the reasons, not the 'why' thereof.

Since there are a multitude of objects concerning which we can have no Experience, for example the past, we are obliged to have recourse to the **Authority** of others. Moreover, these objects which we hold for true upon the Authority of others are objects of Experience (i.e. empirical objects). We *believe* them upon the Authority of others which is probable. We often hold as probable that which is really improbable and what is improbable often turns out to be the truth. (An event receives its confirmation chiefly through its results and through the manifold circumstances connected with our experience of it. Those who narrate to us an event must be *trustworthy*, that is, they must have been in a position where it was possible for them to have knowledge of it. We draw conclusions from the tone and manner in which they relate the event, in regard to their degree of earnestness or the selfish purpose subserved by it. When writers, under the reign of a tyrant, are lavish in his praises, we at once pronounce them to be flatterers. But if one makes special mention of a good quality or deed of his enemy we are the more ready to believe his statements.)

Experience, therefore, teaches only how objects *are* constituted and not how they *must* be or how they *ought* to be. This latter knowledge comes only from a concept of the Essence or Idea of the object, a knowledge of it as a whole. And this latter knowledge alone is true knowledge. Since we must learn the grounds of an object from its Concept, a knowledge of it in its entire compass, so too, if we would learn the character of the Lawful, Moral and Religious, we must have recourse to the Concepts thereof.

In determining what is right and good we may at first hold to Experience and that too of the most external kind, namely, the way of the world. We can see there what passes for right and good or what proves itself to be right and good. Upon this phase it is to be remarked (a) that in order to know what deeds are right or good and what are wrong or wicked, one presupposes himself to be in possession of the Concept of the **Right [Lawful]** and **Good** and (b) if anyone chose to hold to that which the way of the world showed to be current as right and good he would not arrive at anything definite. All would depend upon the view with which he undertook the investigation. In the course of the world, wherein there occurs such a variety of events, each one can find his own particular view justified be it ever so peculiar.

But there is, secondly, an *internal* experience concerning the Right [Legal], Good and Religious. We judge upon our **Sentiment** [*Gemüt*] or **Feeling** [*Gefühl*] that a deed of this or that character is good or bad. Moreover, we have a Feeling of Religion; we are affected religiously. What Feeling says of the deed by way of *approval* or *disapproval* contains merely the immediate expression, or the mere assurance, that something is so or is not so. Feeling gives no reasons for its decision, nor does it decide with reference to reasons. What kind of Feeling we have, of approval or of disapproval, is the mere *experience* of a Sentiment. Feeling is, however, inconstant and changeable. It is at one time in one state and at another in a different one. Feeling is, in short, something *subjective*. An object of Feeling is my object as a particular individual. If I say: 'I feel thus about it' or 'It is my *sentiment* toward it', I then say only what belongs to me as an individual. I leave undecided whether it is also the same in other persons. When I, upon any occasion, appeal simply to my Feeling, I do not desire to enter upon the reasons [and] consequently upon universal relations. I withdraw myself within myself and express only what concerns me and not what is in-and-for-itself objective and universal. The **Objective**, or the universal, is the **Intelligible**, or the **Concept [Notion]**.

If anyone wishes to know truly what a rose or a pink or an oak is, that is, if he wishes to grasp it in its Concept [or Idea], he must first grasp the higher Concept which lies at its base, namely that of *Plant*; and further, in order to grasp the Concept of the 'plant', one must again grasp the higher Concept whereupon the Concept of the 'plant' depends, and this is the Concept of an *Organic Body*. In order to have the representation [idea] of bodies, surfaces, lines, and points, one must have recourse to the Concept of Space, since Space is the *generic* thereof; hence bodies, surfaces, etc. are only particular determinations of Space. In the same manner the present, past and future presuppose Time as their generic ground. And so it is with Laws, Duties and Religion; they are merely particular determinations of Consciousness, which is their generic ground.

3

In the first stage of Consciousness we are usually aware of the object before us, that is, we are aware only of the object not of ourselves. But it is essentially in these things that the 'I' [Ego] exists. In so far as we think simply of an object we have a Consciousness, that is, a consciousness of the object. In so far as we think of Consciousness we are conscious of Consciousness, that is, we have a consciousness of Consciousness. In our ordinary life we have consciousness but we are not conscious that we are a Consciousness; there is much in use that is even corporeal of which we are *unconscious*; for example, the vital functions which minister to our self-preservation we possess without being conscious of their precise constitution, this we only acquire through Science. Also, from a spiritual standpoint, we are much more than we know. The *external* objects of our Consciousness are those which we distinguish from ourselves and to which we ascribe an independent existence. The *inner* objects, on the other hand, are determinations or faculties, [i.e.] powers of the Ego. They do not subsist in separation from one another but only in the Ego. Consciousness functions *theoretically* or *practically*.

4

Theoretical Consciousness considers that which is and leaves it as it is. Practical [Consciousness], on the other hand, is the active consciousness which does not leave what is as it is but produces changes therein and produces from itself determinations and objects. In Consciousness, therefore, two things are present: myself and the object; I am determined by the object or the object is determined by me. In the former case my relationship is *theoretical* [and in the latter case *practical*]. [In Theoretical Consciousness] I take up the determinations of the object as *they are*. I leave the object as it is and seek to make my ideas conform to it. I have determinations in myself and the object also has determinations within it. The content of the Idea about the object should conform to what the object is. The determinations of the object in-itself are rules for me. The truth of my Ideas consists in their correspondence with the constitution and the determinations of the object. The law for our Consciousness, in so far as it is *theoretical*, is that it must not be completely passive but must direct its activity to receiving the object. Something can be an object for our perception without our having on that account a consciousness of it when we do not direct our activity to it. This activity in reception is called **Attention**.

5

The Ideas which we acquire through Attention we excite in ourselves through the power of **Imagination**, whose activity consists in this: that it calls up in connection with the intuition of one object the image of another in some way or other linked with it. It is not necessary that the object, to which the Imagination links the image of another, be present; it may be present only in an idea of it. The most extensive work of the Imagination is **Language**. Language consists in external signs and sounds through which one makes known what he thinks, feels or senses. Language consists in **Words**, which are nothing else than signs of thoughts. For these signs there are again found in writing other signs called letters. They make known our thoughts without our having to speak them. *Hieroglyphic* writing is distinguished from the *Alphabetic* by its direct presentation of *entire thoughts*.★
In **Speech** a certain sound is sensuously present and therein we have the intuition of a sound. But we do not stop at this because our Imagination links to it the idea of an absent object. Here then we have two different objects, a sensuous determination and another idea linked to it. Here the idea counts solely as the essence and as the meaning of what is sensuously present which is thus a mere sign. The *given* content confronts a content which we have *produced*.

6

In ordinary life, the expressions *to have an Idea* and *to Think* [*vorstellen* as opposed to *denken*] are used *interchangeably* and we thus dignify

★ *Translator's Note*: Though this passage was written before the Rosetta Stone was discovered and is therefore no longer valid in respect of Egyptian hieroglyphs, Hegel's comments are still valid for other Asiatic forms of hieroglyphic writing.

with the name of thought what is only the product of imagination. In 'Ideas' of this sort we have an object before us in its external and unessential existence. In **Thinking**, on the contrary, we separate from the object its external, merely unessential side, and consider the object merely in its essence. Thinking penetrates through the external phenomenon to the internal nature of the thing and makes it its object. It leaves the contingent side of the thing out of consideration. It takes up a subject not as it is in immediate appearance, but severs the unessential from the essential and thus abstracts from it. In **Intuition** we have single objects before us. Thinking brings them into *relation* with each other or *compares* them. In **Comparison** it singles out what they have in common with each other and omits that by which they differ and thus it retains only universal ideas. The universal Idea contains less determinateness than the single object which belongs under this universal, since one arrives at the universal only by leaving out something from the single thing; on the other hand, the universal *includes* more under it or has a much greater extension. In so far as Thinking produces a universal object, the activity of abstracting belongs to it and hence it has the Form of the universal (as, for example, in the universal object 'Man'.) But the content of the universal object does not belong to it as an activity of abstracting but is given to Thinking and is independent of it and present on its own account.

To Thinking there belong manifold determinations which express a *connection* between the manifold phenomena that is *universal* and *necessary*. The connection as it exists in Sensuous Intuition is merely an external or contingent one, which may or may not be in any particular form. A stone, for example, makes by its fall an impression upon a yielding mass. In the Sensuous Intuition is contained the fact of the falling of the stone and the fact of an impression made in the yielding mass where the stone touched it. These two phenomena, the falling of the stone and the impression on the yielding mass, have a succession in time. But this connection contains, as yet, no necessity: on the contrary it is possible, for all that is therein stated, that the one might have happened under the same conditions without the other following it. When, on the contrary, the relation of these two phenomena to each other is determined as cause and effect, or as the relation of **Causality**, then this connection is a necessary one or a connection of the Understanding. This entails that under the same conditions, if one happens, the other is contained in it.

These determinations are the forms of Thinking. The Mind posits them solely through *its own activity* but they are at the same time *determinations of existing things* [*zugleich Bestimmungen des Seienden*]. We come first by Reflection to distinguish what is Ground and Consequent, Internal and External, Essential and Unessential. The Mind is not at first conscious that it posits these determinations by its own free will, but thinks that it [Mind] expresses in them [these determinations] something which is present without its assistance.

7

Whenever we speak of the Ego or the Mind as receiving determinations we presuppose its previous indeterminateness. The determinations of the Mind always belong to the Mind even though it has received them from other objects. Although something may be in the Mind which came from without as a content not dependent upon the Mind, yet the form always belongs to the latter; e.g. although in the Imagination the material may be derived from Sensuous Intuition, the *form* consists in the method in which this material is combined in a different manner from that present in the original intuition. In a pure Concept, e.g. that of animal, the specific content belongs to Experience but the universal element in it is the form which comes from the Mind.

This form is thus of the Mind's own determining. The essential difference between the *theoretical* and the *practical* functions of the Mind consists in this: that in the theoretical the form alone is determined by the Mind while, on the other hand, in the practical function the content also proceeds from the Mind. In Right, for example, the content is personal freedom. This belongs to the Mind. The practical function recognizes determinations as its own in so far as it wills them. Even if they are alien determinations, or given from without, they must cease to be alien in so far as *I* will them: I change the content into *mine* and posit it through myself.

8

Theoretical Activity starts from something externally present and converts it into an Idea. **Practical Activity**, on the other hand, starts from an internal determination. This is called resolve, intention, or direction and makes the internal actually external and gives to it existence. This transition from an internal determination to externality is called **Act**.

9

The Act is, in general terms, a union of the *internal* and *external*. The internal determination, from which it begins, has to be cancelled and made external as far as its form is concerned, which form is that of a mere internal. The content of this determination is still to remain [after negation of the form]; e.g. the intention to build a house is an internal determination whose form consists in this: that it is only an intention at first; the content includes the plan of the house. If the form now is here cancelled, the content will still remain. The house which is to be built according to the intention and that which is built according to the plan are the same house.

Conversely, the Act is likewise a sublation of externality as it is immediately present; e.g. the building of a house necessitates a change in a variety of ways, of the ground, the building-stone, the wood, and the other materials. The shape of the external is changed; it is brought into quite other combinations than existed before. These changes happen in conformity to a purpose, to wit, the plan of the house with which internal something the external is to be made to harmonize.

10

Animals, too, stand in a practical relation to that which is external to them. They act from instinct, with designs and purposes to realize, and thus rationally. Since they do this unconsciously, however, we cannot properly speak of them as authors of Voluntary Acts. They have Desires and Impulses, but no Rational Will. In speaking of man's impulses and desires, it is usual to include the Will. But, more accurately speaking, the Will is to be distinguished from Desire. The Will, in distinction from Desire, is called the **Higher Appetite**. With animals even **Instinct** is to be distinguished from their impulses and desires, for though Instinct is an acting from Impulse and Desire it, however, does not terminate with its immediate externalization but has a further, and for the animal likewise necessary, result. It is an acting in which there is involved also a relation to something else; e.g. the hoarding up of grain by many animals. This is not yet quite properly to be called an Act, but it contains a design in it, namely, provision for the future.

Impulse is, in the first place, something *internal*, something which begins a movement from itself, or produces a change by its own power. Impulse proceeds from itself. Although it may be awakened by external circumstances, yet it existed already without regard to them; it is not produced by them. Mechanical causes produce mere external or mechanical effects which are completely determined by their causes, in which therefore nothing is contained which is not already present in the cause; e.g. if I give motion to a body, the motion imparted to it is all that it has, or if I paint a body, it has nothing else than the colour imparted to it. On the contrary, if I act upon a living creature my influence upon it becomes something quite different from what it was in me. The activity of the living creature is aroused by my act and it exhibits its own peculiarity in reacting against it.

In the second place, Impulse is (a) *limited* in respect to content [and] (b) is *contingent* as regards the aspect of its gratification, since it is dependent upon external circumstances. Impulse does not transcend its purpose [end] and is therefore spoken of as blind. It gratifies itself, let the consequences be what they may.

Man does not make his own Impulses, he simply has them; in other words, they belong to his nature. Nature is, however, under the rule of necessity because everything in Nature is limited, relative or exists only in relation to something else. But what exists only in relation to something else is not for-itself but dependent upon others. It has its ground in that [something else] and is a *necessitated* being. In so far as man has immediately determined Impulses he is subjected to Nature, and conducts himself as a necessitated and unfree being.

11

But man can, as a thinking being, *reflect* upon his impulses which have in themselves necessity for him. **Reflection** signifies, in general, the cutting off from or reduction [*Abkürzung*] of the immediate. Reflection (in respect of light) consists in this, that the rays [of light] which, in-themselves, beam forth in straight lines are bent back from this direction. Mind has Reflection. It is not confined to the immediate but may transcend it and proceed to something else; e.g. from the event before it, it may proceed to form an idea of its consequences or of a similar event or also of its causes. When the Mind goes out to something immediate it has removed the same from itself. It has reflected itself into itself. *It has gone into itself*. It has recognized the immediate as a *conditioned*, or *limited*, in as much as it opposes to it another. It is, therefore, a very great difference whether one *is* or *has* something and whether he *knows* that he is or has it; for example, ignorance or rudeness of the sentiments or of behaviour are limitations which one may have without knowing it. In so far as one reflects or knows of them he must know of their opposite. Reflection upon them is already a first step beyond them.

Impulses, as natural determinations, are limitations. Through reflection upon them man begins to transcend them. The first Reflection concerns the *means*, whether they are commensurate with the impulse, whether the impulse will be gratified through the means; whether, in the second place, the means are not too important to be sacrificed for this impulse. Reflection compares the different impulses and their purposes with the fundamental end and purpose of Being. The purposes of the special impulses are limited but they contribute, each in its own way, to the attainment of the fundamental purpose. One, however, is better adapted for this than another. Hence Reflection has to compare impulses and ascertain which are more closely allied to the fundamental purpose and are best adapted to aid its realization by their gratification. In Reflection begins the transition from lower forms of appetite to the higher. Man is, in Reflection, no longer a mere natural being and stands no longer in the sphere of necessity. Something is necessary when only this and not something else can happen. Reflection has before it not only the one immediate object but also another or its opposite.

12

This Reflection just described is, however, a merely *relative* affair. Although it transcends the finite, yet it always arrives again at the finite; e.g. when we exceed the limits of one place in space there rises before us another portion of space, greater than before, but it is always only a finite space that thus arises, *ad infinitum*. Likewise, when we go back in time beyond the present into the past we can imagine a period of ten thousand or thirty thousand years. Though such reflection proceeds from one particular point in space or time to another, yet it never gets beyond space or time. Such is also the case in the Reflection which is both practical and relational. It leaves some one immediate inclination, desire or impulse and proceeds to another one, and in the end abandons this one also. In so far as it is relative it only falls again into another impulse, moves round and round in a circle of appetites and does not elevate itself above the sphere of impulses as a whole.

The *practical* **Absolute Reflection**, however, does elevate itself above this entire sphere of the finite; in other words, it abandons the sphere of the lower appetites, in which man is determined by nature and dependent on the outside world. **Finitude** consists, on the whole, in this: that something has a limit, i.e., that *here its non-being* is posited or that here it stops, that through this limit it is related to an 'other'. Infinite Reflection, however, consists, in this: that the Ego is no longer related to another, but is related to itself; in other words is its own object. This pure relation to myself is the **Ego**, the root of the Infinite Being itself. It is the perfect abstraction from all that is finite.

The Ego as such has no content which is immediate, i.e. given to it by nature, but its sole content is itself. *This pure Form is, at the same time, its content*: (a) every content given by nature is something limited: but the Ego is unlimited; (b) the content given by nature is immediate: the pure Ego, however, has no immediate content for the reason that the pure Ego only is by means of the complete abstraction from everything else.

13

In the first place the Ego is the purely indeterminate. It is able, however, by means of reflection, to pass over from indeterminateness to determinateness, e.g. to seeing, hearing, etc. In this determinateness it has become *non-self-identical*, but it has still remained in its indeterminateness; i.e. it is able, at will, to withdraw into itself again. At this place enters the **Act of Resolving** [Volition] for Reflection precedes it and consists in this; that the Ego has before it several determinations indefinite as to number and yet each of these must be in one of two predicaments: it necessarily is or is not a determination of the something under consideration. The Act of Resolution cancels that of Reflection, the process to and fro from one to the other, and fixes on a determinateness and makes it its own. The fundamental condition necessary to the Act of Resolving, the possibility of *making up one's mind* to do something or even of reflecting prior to the act, is the absolute indeterminateness of the Ego.

14

The **Freedom of the Will** is freedom in general, and all other *freedoms* are mere species thereof. When the expression 'Freedom of the Will' is used, it is not meant that apart from the Will there is a force or property or faculty which possesses freedom. Just as when the omnipotence of God is spoken of it is not understood that there are still other beings besides him who possess omnipotence. There is also civil freedom, freedom of the press, political and religious freedom. These species of freedom belong to the universal concept of Freedom in so far as it applies to special objects. **Religious Freedom** consists in this: that religious ideas, religious deeds, are not forced upon me, that is, that there are in them only such determinations as I recognize as my own and make my own. A religion which is forced upon me, or in relation to which I cannot act as a free being, is not my own, but remains alien to me. The **Political Freedom** of a people consists in this: that they form for themselves their own State and decide what is to be valid as the national will, and that this be done either by the whole people themselves or by those who belong to the people, and who, since every other citizen has the same rights as themselves, can be acknowledged by the people as their own [i.e. as their representatives].

15

Such expressions as these are often used: 'My will has been determined by these motives, circumstances, incitements, or inducements.' This expression implies that I have stood in a *passive* relation [to these motives, etc.]. In truth, however, the Ego did not stand in a merely passive relation but was essentially active therein. The Will, that is, accepted these circumstances as motives and allowed them validity as motives. The causal relation here does not apply. The circumstances do not stand in the relation of cause nor my Will in that of effect. In the causal relation the effect follows necessarily when the cause is given. As reflection, however, I can transcend each and every determination which is posited by the circumstances. In so far as a man pleads in his defence that he was led astray through circumstances, incitements, etc. and, by this plea, [hopes] to rid himself of the consequences of his deed, he lowers himself to the state of an unfree, natural being; while, in truth, his deed is always his own and not that of another or the effect of something outside himself. Circumstances or motives have only so much control over man as he himself gives to them.

The determinations of the Lower Appetites are natural determinations. In so far, it seems to be neither necessary nor possible for man to make them his own. Simply as natural determinations they do not belong to his Will or to his freedom, for the essence of his Will is that nothing be in it which he has not made his own. He, therefore, is able to regard what belongs to his nature as something alien, so that, consequently, it is only in him, only belongs to him in so far as he makes it his own or follows with his volition his natural impulses.

16

To hold a man responsible for an Act means to impute or attribute to him guilt or innocence. Children who are still in a state of nature cannot be held responsible for their deeds, nor can crazy people or idiots.

17

In the distinction of **Deed** from **Act** [*Tat* and *Handlung*] lies the distinction between the ideas of moral responsibility as they are presented in the tragedies of the ancients and those current in our own time. In the former, among the ancients, Deed was attributed in its entire extent to man. He had to do penance for the *entire* compass of his actions and no distinction was made if he was conscious of only one aspect of his act and unconscious of the others. He was considered as having an absolute knowledge and not [merely] a relative and contingent knowledge, [in that] whatever he did was considered as his *own* Deed. Part of him was referred to another Being; e.g. Ajax, when he slew the oxen and sheep of the Greeks in a state of insanity and rage caused by his not receiving the arms of Achilles, did not attribute his crime to his madness, as though he were another being while insane, but he took the whole deed upon himself as its author and slew himself from shame.

18

If the Will were not *universal* there could be, properly speaking, no actual statutes and nothing which could be imposed as obligatory upon *all*. Each one could act according to his own pleasure and would not respect the pleasure of others. That the Will is universal flows from the concept of its freedom. Men, considered as they are in the world, show themselves very different in character, customs, inclinations and particular sentiments that is, they differ in their Will. They are by this *different* individuals and differ by nature from each other. Each one has natural abilities and determinations which others lack. These differences between individuals do not concern the Will in itself, for it is free. Freedom consists precisely in the indeterminateness of the Will or in the fact that it has no determined nature in it. The Will by itself is thus a Universal Will. The particularity or individuality of man does not stand in the way of the universality of the Will but is subordinated to it. An Act which is good legally or morally, although done by some one individual, is assented to by all others. They thus recognize themselves, or their own wills, in it. It is the same case here as with works of art. Even those who could never produce such a work find expressed in it their own nature. Such a work shows itself, therefore, as truly universal. It receives the greater applause the less it exhibits the idiosyncrasy of its author.

It can be the case that one is unconscious of his Universal Will. He may believe, indeed, that it is directly opposed to his Will, even though it is his [true] Will. The criminal who is punished may wish, of course, that the punishment be warded off but the Universal Will brings with it the decree that the criminal shall be punished. It must be assumed that the Absolute Will of the criminal *demands* that he shall be punished. In so far as he is punished the demand is made that he shall see that he is punished justly and, if he sees this, although he may wish to be freed from the punishment as an external suffering yet, in so far as he concedes that he is justly punished, his Universal Will approves of the punishment.

19

The **Will-of-Choice [Arbitrariness]** is freedom, but only *formal* freedom or freedom in so far as one's Will relates to something limited. Two aspects must here be distinguished: (a) in how far the Will does not remain identical with itself in it and (b) in how far it does remain so.

(a) In so far as the Will wills *something* it has a determined, limited content. It is, in so far, non-identical with itself because it is here actually determined, although in-and-for-itself it is undetermined. The limited content which it has taken up is therefore something else than it itself; e.g. if I will to go or to see, I become a going or a seeing one. I thus enter a relation not identical to myself, since the going and seeing is something limited and not identical with the Ego.

(b) But in relation to the Form I stand in identity with myself or am free still, since I, all the while, distinguish this state of determination from myself as something *alien*, for the acts of going and seeing are not posited in me by nature but by myself in my own will. In so far as this is the case it is evidently no alien affair because it is made my own and I have my own will in it.

This freedom is only formal freedom because, together with my *self-identity*, there is present also, at the same time, *non-identity* with myself or, in other words, there is a limited content in the Ego. When in common life we speak of freedom, we ordinarily understand, under the expression caprice or relative freedom, the liberty to do or to refrain from doing something or other. In the limited Will we can have formal freedom in so far as we distinguish the particular content of our Will from ourselves or reflect upon it, that is, in so far as we are also beyond and above it. If we are in a passion or if we act through a natural impulse we have no formal freedom. Since our Ego, in this emotion, gives itself up wholly it seems to us to be something unlimited [or infinite]. Our Ego is not out[side] of it and does not separate itself from it.

20

The **Absolute Free Will** distinguishes itself from the **Relatively Free Will** or **Will-of-Choice [Arbitrariness]** through this: the Absolute Will has only itself for object, while the Relative Will has something limited. With the Relative Will, with, for example, the appetite, the object of that Will [its content] is all that concerns it. But the Absolute [Will] must be carefully distinguished from **Wilfulness**. The latter has this in common with the Absolute Will: that it concerns itself not merely with the object but also with the will as Will, insisting that its will as such shall be respected. A distinction is here to be made. The stubborn [wilful] man insists on his will simply because it is his will, without offering a rational ground for it, i.e. without showing his will to have general validity. While strength of will is necessary, such as holds unwaveringly by a rational purpose, on the other hand mere stubbornness, such as arises from idiosyncrasy and is repulsive toward others, is to be detested. The true Free Will has no contingent content. It alone is not contingent.

21

The **Pure Will** has nothing to do with particularity. In so far as particularity comes into the Will it is Arbitrariness, for Arbitrariness has a limited interest and takes its determinations from natural impulses and inclinations. Such a content is a given one and is not posited absolutely through the will. The fundamental principle of the Will is, therefore, that its freedom be established and preserved. Besides this it has indeed many different kinds of determinations: it has a variety of definite purposes, regulations, conditions, etc., but these are not purposes of the Will in-and-for-itself. Still they are purposes for the reason that they are *means* and *conditions* for the *realization* of the freedom of the Will, which [realization] demands regulations and laws for the purpose of restraining caprice and inclination or mere 'good pleasure'. In a word, the impulses and appetites which relate to mere natural ends, e.g. **Education**, has for its end the elevation of man to an independent state of existence: i.e. to that existence wherein he is a Free Will. On this view many restraints are imposed upon the desires and likings of children. They must learn to obey and consequently to annul their mere individual or particular wills and, moreover, [to annul also] to this end their sensuous inclinations and appetites that, by this means, their Will may become free.

22

Firstly, Man is a free being. This constitutes the fundamental characteristic of his nature. Nevertheless, besides freedom he has other necessary wants, special purposes and impulses, e.g. the impulse for knowledge, for the preservation of his life, health, etc. In these special determinations Law has not man as such for its object. It has not the design to further him in the pursuit of the same or to afford him special help therein.

Secondly, Law does not depend upon one's *motives*. One may do something with the best of intentions and yet the deed be not lawful and just for all this but wrong. On the other hand an act, for example the maintenance of my property, may be perfectly lawful and yet I have a bad motive since I may have sought not what was just and lawful but the injury of another. Upon Law as such the intention or motive has no influence.

Thirdly, it is not a matter of conviction as to whether that which I perform is right or wrong. This holds particularly with regard to punishment. Although an effort is made to convince the criminal that he has violated what is Law, yet his conviction or non-conviction has no influence on the justice that is meted out to him.

Finally, Law pays no regard to the *disposition* or sentiment under whose influence anything is done. It very often happens that one does what is right merely through fear of punishment or fear of unpleasant consequences, such, for instance, as the loss of reputation or credit. Or it happens that one does right from the conviction that he will be rewarded in another life. Law, however, as such, is independent of these sentiments and convictions.

23

Law must be distinguished from **Morality**. Something may be well enough from a legal point of view which is not allowable from a moral point of view. The Law grants me the disposition of my property without determining how I shall dispose of it, but Morality contains determinations which restrain me in this respect. It may seem as though Morality permitted many things which the Law does not, but Morality demands not merely the observance of Justice towards others but requires also that the disposition to do right shall be present, that the law shall be respected as Law. Morality demands first that the legal right shall be obeyed and where it ceases enters moral determination.

In order that an act may have moral value *insight* is necessary into its nature [as to] whether it be right or wrong, good or evil. What one terms the innocence of children or of uncivilized nations is not yet Morality. Children or such uncivilized nations escape the commission of a multitude of bad acts because they have no ideas of them: i.e. because the essential relations are not yet extant under which alone such deeds are possible. Such non-committal of evil acts has no moral value. But they do perform acts which are not in accordance with Morality and yet, for the reason that no insight exists into their nature [as to] whether they are good or bad, they are not strictly Moral acts.

Private conviction stands opposed to the mere faith in the *authority of another*. If my act is to have moral value my conviction must enter into the act. The act must be mine in a whole sense. If I act on the authority of another my act is not fully my own; it is the act of an alien conviction in me.

There are, however, relations in which the moral aspect consists precisely in being *obedient* and acting according to the authority of another. Originally man followed his natural inclinations without reflection or else with reflections that were one-sided, wrong, unjust and under the dominion of the senses. In this condition the best thing for him was to learn to obey, for the reason that his will was not yet a rational one. Through this obedience the negative advantage is gained that he learns to renounce his sensuous appetites and only through such obedience can Man attain to independence and freedom. In this sphere he always follows another, whether it be his own will, still immersed in the senses, or whether it be the will of another. As a natural creature he stands under the dominion of external things and his inclinations and appetites are something immediate [and] not free or something alien to his true will. The one who is obedient to the Law of Reason is obedient from the point of view of his *unessential* nature only, which stands under the dominion of that which is alien to him. On the other hand he is independent self-determination, for this Law has its root in his essence.

The **Disposition** [*Gesinnung*] is thus in the moral realm an essential element. It consists in this: that one does his duty for its own sake. It is, therefore, an immoral motive to do anything out of fear of punishment or in order to preserve another's good opinion. This is a heterogeneous motive, for it is not from the nature of the thing itself. In such a case one does not consider the Law as something in-and-for-itself but as dependent upon external determinations.

Yet the consideration whether an action is to be punished or rewarded, although the consequences do not constitute the value of a deed, is of importance. The consequences of a good act may sometimes involve much that is evil and, on the contrary, an evil act involve much good. The thinking upon the consequences of an act is important, for the reason that one does not remain standing by an immediate point of view but proceeds beyond it. Through its manifold consideration one is led to the nature of Acts.

According to the standpoint of Law man is his own object as an absolutely free existence; according to the moral standpoint on the contrary he is self-object, an individual in his special existence, a member of the family, a friend, a particular character, etc. If the external circumstances in which one man stands with another are so situated that he fulfils his vocation, that is his **Fortune**. This well-being depends partly on his own will and partly upon external circumstances and other men. Morality has, also, the particular existence or well-being of man for its object and demands not only that man be left in his abstract freedom but that his happiness be promoted. Well-being, as the adaptation of the external to our internal being, we call **Pleasure**. **Happiness** is not a mere individual pleasure but an enduring condition [which is] in part the actual Pleasure itself [and], in part also, the circumstances and means through which one always has, at will, the ability to create a state of comfort and pleasure for himself. The latter form is the pleasure of the mind. In Happiness, however, as in Pleasure, there lies the idea of good fortune [good luck]: that it is an accidental matter whether or no the external circumstances agree with the internal determinations of the desires. **Blessedness**, on the contrary, consists in this: that no fortune [luck] pertains to it: i.e. that in it the agreement of the external existence with the internal desire is not accidental. Blessedness can be predicated only of God, in whom willing and accomplishment of his absolute power is the same. For man, however, the harmony of the external with his internal is limited and contingent. In this he is dependent.

24

The **Moral Will**, in regard to its disposition and conviction, is imperfect. It is a Will which *aims at perfection* but (a) is driven towards the attainment of the same through the impulses of sensuousness and individuality and (b) has not the adequate means in its power and is, therefore, limited to bringing about the good of others.

In **Religion**, on the contrary, we consider the Divine Being the perfection of the Will, according to its two aspects, namely [a] the *perfection of the disposition* which no longer has any alien impulses within and [b] the *perfection of the power* to attain holy ends [or purposes].

OUTLINES OF THE SCIENCE OF LAWS, MORALS AND RELIGION

FIRST PART
SCIENCE OF LAW

1

Law must be considered:

(1) in its Essence,
(2) in its Actual Existence in Political Society.

CHAPTER 1
LAW

2

According to Law the Universal Will should have full sway without regard to what may be the intention or conviction of the individual. Law applies to man only in so far as he is a wholly free being.

3

Law consists in this: that each individual be respected and treated by the other as a free being; for only under this condition can the free Will have itself as object and content in the other.

Explanatory: The freedom of the individual lies at the basis of Law and the Law consists in this: that I treat the other as a free being. Reason demands lawful behaviour. Essentially, every man is a free being. Men differ from each other in their special conditions and peculiarities but this difference does not concern the **Abstract Will** as such. In the Abstract Will all are the same and when a man respects another he respects himself. It follows that by the violation of the rights of *one* individual the rights of *all* are violated. This sympathy with others is quite a different thing from the sympathy which one feels at another's *misfortune*. For, although the injury or loss which a man suffers in gifts of fortune (which gifts though desirable are not in themselves essential) concerns me, yet I cannot say that it absolutely ought not to have happened. Such misfortunes belong to the particularity of man. In all our sympathy we separate misfortunes from ourselves and look upon them as something apart from us. On the other hand, at the infringement of another's rights each one feels himself attacked, because Law is something universal. Hence a violation of the Law cannot be looked upon as something foreign [*fremdes*]. We ourselves feel such an infringement all the more, for the Law is necessary.

4

In so far as each man is recognized and acknowledged as a free being, he is a **Person**. The proposition of the Law is therefore to be expressed thus: Each should be treated by the other as a Person.
Explanatory: The concept of Personality includes in itself selfhood or individuality which is free or universal. People have Personality through their spiritual nature.

5

It follows, hence, that no man can justly be compelled except for the purpose of annulling the constraint which he has placed upon others.
Explanatory: There are limitations of freedom and law which permit people to be treated not as persons but as chattels, e.g. the laws which permit slavery. These are, however, only positive laws or rights, which are opposed to Reason or Absolute Right.

6

That action which limits the freedom of another or does not acknowledge and treat him as a free will is illegal.
Explanatory: In an absolute sense no constraint is possible against man because he is a free being and can assert his will against necessity and can give up all that belongs to his existence. Constraint takes place when some condition is attached to a man's existence in such a way that, if he would maintain his existence, he must submit to the condition. Since man's existence is dependent upon external objects, in that respect, he is liable to alien interferences. Man is externally constrained only when he wills something which involves another; it depends upon his will whether he will have *one* and with it *the other* or *neither of them*. The external constraint, of course, depends upon his will, that is, in how far he places himself under it. Hence the external constraint is only relative. It is *legal* constraint when it is exercised for the purpose of enforcing justice *against* the individual. This species of constraint has an aspect according to which it is not a constraint and does not contradict the dignity of a free being, for the reason that the Will in-and-for-itself is also the Absolute Will of each individual. Freedom is not found where the arbitrary will or caprice of the individual [dominates] but where Law prevails.

7

Permitted, but not for this reason *commanded*, is the legal aspect of all actions that do not limit the freedom of another or annul another's act.

Explanatory: The Law contains properly only prohibitions and no commandments. What is not expressly forbidden is allowed. Of course legal prohibitions can be positively expressed as commands, as for instance: 'Thou shalt keep thy contract.' The general legal principle, of which all others are only special applications, reads thus: 'Thou shalt leave undisturbed the property of another.' This does not require anything positive to be done or a change of circumstances to be produced but requires only the *abstention from the violation* of property. When, therefore, the Law is expressed as a positive command, this is only a form of expression, the content of which is always based on a prohibition.

8

The Will, when it subsumes a thing under itself, makes it its own. **Possession** is the subsumption of a thing under my will.

Explanatory: To the subsumption of something there belong two parts: one universal and the other individual. I subsume something individual when I attribute to it a universal determination. This subsumption occurs in the **Act of Judgement**. In the Judgement that which subsumes is the **Predicate** and that which is subsumed is the **Subject**. The 'act of taking possession' is the expression of the Judgement that a thing becomes mine. Here my will is that which subsumes. I give to the thing the predicate that it is mine. The will is the subsuming activity for all external things, since it is in itself the universal essence. All things which are however, not self-related are only necessitated and not free. This fact gives man the right to take possession of all external things and to make of them something different from what they are. In doing so he treats them only in conformity with their essence.

9

(1) The thing which one takes possession of for the first time must be *res nullius*, i.e. not already subsumed under another will.

Explanatory: A thing which already belongs to another cannot be taken possession of by me, not because it is a chattel, but because it is *his* chattel. For were I to take possession of the chattel I would then annul its predicate to be *his* and thereby negate his will. The Will is something absolute and I cannot make it something negative.

10

(2) Property must be openly taken possession of [*ergiffen*], that is, it must be made known to others that I will to subsume this object under my will, be it through *physical seizure* [*körperliche Ergreifung*] or through *transformation* [*Formierung*] or at least by *designation* of the object.

Explanatory: The external seizure must be preceded by the internal act of the will which expresses that the thing is to be mine. The first kind of appropriation is that of **Physical Seizure**. It has this defect, that the objects to be seized must be so constituted that I can take hold of them with the hand or cover them with my body and, furthermore, that the appropriation is not [a] permanent [one]. The second, more complete kind of appropriation, is that of **Transforming** [*Formierung*] a thing, as for example cultivating a field [and] making gold into a cup. In this case the *form* of what is mine is directly connected with the object and is, therefore, in and for itself a sign that the *material* also belongs to me. To this kind [of taking possession] belongs, among other things, the planting of trees [and the] taming and feeding of animals. An imperfect form of property in land is the use of a territory without its cultivation: e.g. when nomadic peoples use territory for pasturage, hunters for hunting grounds [and] fishermen the sea coast or river bank for their purposes. Such an appropriation is still superficial because the actual use is only a temporary one [and] not a permanent form of possession closely attached to the object. Appropriation by merely **Designation** of the object is imperfect. That designation which does not, as in an improvement, constitute the essential nature of the thing is a mere external affair; what meaning it has is more or less foreign to its own essence but it also has, as well, a meaning peculiarly it own which is not connected with the nature of the thing designated. The designation is thus arbitrary. It is more or less a matter of convenience what the designation of a thing shall be.

11

A Possession becomes **Property** or a **Legal [Possession]** when it is acknowledged by everyone else that the thing which I have made mine is mine, just as I acknowledge the Property of others as theirs. My possession is *acknowledged* for the reason that it is an act of the free will, which is something absolute in itself [and] in which lies the universal [condition] that I regard the will of others as something absolute.

Explanatory: Possession and Property are two different determinations. It is not necessary that Possession and Property be always connected. It is possible for me to have Property without being in Possession of it. When, for example, I lend something to another the property still remains mine though I part with the possession of it. Possession and Property are implied in the concept that I have **Dominium** [i.e. control or dominion] over something. Property is the legal side of the Dominium and Possession is only the external side, namely that something is in my power. The legal right is the side of my absolute free will which has declared something to be someone else's. This will must be acknowledged by others because it is in-and-for-itself and, in so far as the already stated conditions have been observed, Property has, therefore, an internal and an external side. The latter, by itself, is the **Appropriation**, the former is the **Act of Will** which must be acknowledged as such. It seems contingent or arbitrary whether the acknowledgement of others should be added to the fact of taking possession. This is necessary, however, for it lies in the nature of the transaction. Acknowledgement is not based on reciprocity. I do not acknowledge your right because you acknowledge mine, nor vice versa, but the ground of this reciprocal acknowledgement is the nature of the transaction itself. I acknowledge the will of others because the will is to be acknowledged *absolutely*.

12

I can **Dispose** of [or **Alienate**] [*entäussern*] *my* property, and it can become the property of another, through an act of my free will.

Explanatory: My Powers and Skills are my property in the most peculiar sense, but they have also an external aspect. Abstractly considered they are external, [that is] in so far as I can distinguish them from myself, the simple Ego. But also in themselves Powers and Skills are single and limited and they do not constitute my essence. My essence, the intrinsic universal, is distinct from these particular determinations. Finally, they are external in their *use*. In the very act of using them I convert them to an external form and the product is some external existence. Power, as such, does not lie in the use thereof but preserves itself notwithstanding that it is externalized and that this, its externalization, has made it a separate existence. This expression of Power is also an externality in so far as it is something limited and finite. In so far as something is my property I have connected it with my will but this connection is not absolute. For if it were my will would necessarily be involved. But I have, in this case, only particularized my will and, because it is free, can overcome this particularity.

13

Those possessions are *inalienable* which are not so much my property as they are constituent elements of my innermost person or essence; such, for example, as the freedom of the will, ethical law, religion, etc.

Explanatory: Only those possessions are alienable which already, by their nature, are of an external character. Personality, for example, cannot be viewed as external to me, for in so far as a man has given up his *personality* he has reduced himself to a thing. But such an alienation would be null and void. For instance, a man would alienate his ethical nature [*Sittlichkeit*] were he to bind himself to another to perform all manner of acts, crimes as well as [morally] indifferent acts. But such a bond would have no binding force because it alienates the freedom of the will and, in the latter, each one must stand for himself. Right or wrong acts belong to him who commits them and, because they are so constituted, I cannot alienate them. Nor can I alienate my *religion*. If a religious community, or even an individual, leaves it for a third party to determine what shall constitute its faith, such an obligation could be set aside by either party. No wrong at least could be done to the party with whom the agreement had been made because what I have given over to him *could never become his property*.

14

On the other hand, I *can* alienate the specific *use* of my mental and bodily energies as well as the chattel which I may possess.

Explanatory: One can alienate only a *limited* use of his powers, since this use, or the circumscribed effect, is distinct from the Power itself. But the *permanent* use, or the effect in its *entire* extent, cannot be distinguished from the Power in-itself. The Power is the *inner* or *universal*, as opposed to its expression. The expressions are an existence in time and space. The Power in-itself is not exhausted in such a single existence and is, moreover, not tied to one of its contingent effects. But, secondly, the Power must act and express itself, otherwise it is not a power. Thirdly, the entire extent of its effects is again, itself, the universal which the Power is. For this reason man cannot alienate the entire use of his powers; he would, in so doing, alienate his personality.

15

An alienation to another involves *my* consent to resign the property to him, and *his* consent to accept it. This twofold consent, in so far as it is reciprocally declared and expressed as valid, is called **Contract** (*Pactum*).

Explanatory: Contract is a special mode by which one becomes the owner of property which already belongs to another. The mode, already explained, of becoming an owner was that of immediate appropriation of some thing that was *res nullius*.

(1) The simplest form of contract is the **Gift-Contract**: in this only one of the parties gives and another receives, no equivalent being returned. A valid donation is a Contract because the wills of both parties must be involved: the one willing to resign the property to the other without receiving an equivalent thereof and the other being willing to receive the property.

(2) The **Exchange-Contract**, [or] **Barter**, consists in this: I give something to another on condition that he gives something of equivalent value [to me]. To this belongs the twofold consent on the part of each: to give something to and to receive something from the other.

(3) **Buying** and **Selling** is a particular kind of exchange, that of goods for money. **Money** is the universal form of goods; hence, as abstract value, it cannot itself be used for the purpose of satisfying a particular want. It is only the universal means by which to satisfy particular needs. The use of money is only a mediated one. A material is not in-and-for-itself Money because it possesses such and such qualities but it becomes Money only by general agreement.

(4) **Rent** consists in this: that I grant to someone my possession or the use of my property while I reserve the ownership to myself. There are two cases: it may happen that the one to whom I have leased something is bound to return the same identical thing or that I have reserved the right to property the same in kind and amount or of equal value.

16

The declaration of will contained in the contract is not sufficient to complete the transfer of my property or labour to another. This transfer, on the basis of the contract, is **Performance**.

Explanatory: My promise in the contract contains the acknowledgement on my part that I have parted with the title to the property and that the other party has acquired title to the same. The piece of property becomes immediately the property of another through the contract in so far as it had its ground in my will. But, if I do not also place the other party in possession in accordance with the contract, to that extent I despoil him of his property. I am therefore bound by the contract to give possession. (Treat here of acquisition by Testament.)

17

An **Encroachment** [Trespass] upon the sphere of my freedom by another may occur (a) through his having my property in his possession *as his own*; i.e. through his claiming it on the ground that he has the right to it and acknowledging, at the same time, that if I, instead of himself, had the right to it he would surrender it to me. In this he respects Law as such and only asserts that in this instance it is on his side. (b) His action may imply that he does not recognize my will at all and consequently violates the law as Law.

Explanatory: The ideas which we have been considering contain the *nature* of legality, its laws, and its *necessity*. But Law is not 'necessary' in the sense that necessity is used when speaking of physical nature, e.g. the necessity which holds the sun in its place. A flower must wholly conform to its nature. If it, for example, does not complete its growth this comes from the intervention of some external influence, not from itself. Spirit, on the contrary, by reason of its freedom, can act in contravention of the laws. Thus there can be contravention of Law itself. A distinction must here be made between (a) **Universal Law**, Law *qua* Law, and (b) **Particular Law** as it relates to the rights of an individual person in a particular matter.

The Universal Law is that [concept] through which everybody, independent of his or her property, is a legal person. A contravention of the law may take the shape of a mere refusal to concede to an individual some particular right, or some particular piece of property. In this case, the Universal Law is not violated. One stands in relation to his opponent as a legal person. Such a 'judgement' can be regarded as a merely *negative* one in which the particular is denied in the predicate, as for example, when I assert 'This stove is not green', I negate merely the predicate of greenness but not thereby all predicates. In the second case of a contravention of the law I assert not only that a particular thing is the property of another but I deny also that he is a legal person. I do not treat him as a person. I do not lay claim to something on the ground that I have a right to it or believe that I have; I violate the law *as* Law. Such a judgement belongs to the kind of judgement called 'infinite'. The infinite judgement negates not only the particular but also the universal of the predicate; e.g. 'This stove is not a whale' or 'it is not memory.' Since not only the particular but also the universal of the predicate is negated nothing remains for the subject. Such judgements are therefore absurd, though correct in form. So, likewise, the violation of law *as* Law is something possible, and indeed also happens, but it is absurd and self-contradictory. Cases of the first kind come under the Civil Law, those of the second kind under the Criminal Law.

18

In the first case [**Civil Law**] the mere explication of the legal grounds is all that is necessary to show to whom the contested particular right belongs. But for the decision of the case between the two contending parties a third party is necessary, one who is free from all interest in the matter, in order to see that the Law as such is carried out.

Explanatory: Under the first case come, therefore, civil disputes. In these the right of another is called into question but on the basis of Law. The two contending parties agree in this, that they recognize the law as Law. The possession is to be given only to him who has the lawful right and not to the one who has influence, power, or is more deserving. The parties differ only in regard to the subsumption of the particular or of the universal. Hence it follows that there is no personal ill-will between the judge and the parties in dispute, either towards the judge by the dissatisfied party or on the part of the judge towards the party whose legal right he has denied. Since no attack is here made against the person, it follows that the party who has illegally seized the property of the other is not punished.

19

The second case [**Criminal Law**], on the other hand, concerns the violation of my personal external freedom, of my life and limb or even of my property, by violence.

Explanatory: The second case concerns the illegal deprivation of my freedom by imprisonment or slavery. I am deprived of natural external freedom when I cannot go where I want to go and [by] similar restrictions. [This case] also includes injury to my life and limb. This is much more important than robbing me of my property. Although life and limb, like property, is something external, my personality is also injured, since in my body is my immediate feeling of self.

20

The constraint which is effected by such an act must not only be removed, i.e. the internal nugatoriness of such an act be exhibited only negatively, but there must be a positive restitution made. (The form of rationality in general must be made valid against it, the universality or equality restored.) Since the perpetrator is a rational being his action implies that it is something universal. 'If you despoil another, you despoil yourself: if you kill anyone then you kill all and yourself. The action is a law which you set up and, in your deed, you have fully recognized its validity.' The perpetrator may therefore himself be subjected to the same form of treatment as that which he has meted out and, in so far, the equality that he has violated may again be restored (*jus talionis*).

Explanatory: **Retaliation** is based on the rational nature of the wrong-doer [and] it consists in this: that the unlawful act must be converted into a lawful one. The unlawful action is indeed a single irrational action. But, since it is performed by a rational being, it is, according to form though not according to content, rational and universal. Furthermore, it is to be considered as a principle or as Law. But, as such, it is valid only for the one who committed it because he alone recognizes it by his action and no one else. He himself, therefore, is essentially subject to this principle or 'Law' and it must be carried out upon him. The injustice which he has done is lawful when visited [back] upon him because through this second action, which he has recognized, equality is restored. This is merely *formal* justice.

21

The Retaliation, however, ought not to be meted out by the injured party or by his relatives, because with them the general regard for Law is bound up at the same time with the contingency of the passions. Retaliation must be lawfully administered by a third party who merely makes valid and executes the universal. In so far it is **Punishment**.

Explanatory: The difference between **Revenge** and **Punishment** is that Revenge is Retaliation in so far as it is carried out by the injured party; Punishment is administered by the judge. Retaliation must be carried out in the form of Punishment because, in the case of revenge, passion has an influence and justice is spoilt by it. Moreover, revenge has the form not of Law but of caprice, since the injured party always acts under the impulse of feeling or of subjective motives. On this account justice, administered as revenge, constitutes a new offence and is felt only as an individual deed and perpetuates itself unreconciled *ad infinitum*.

CHAPTER 2
POLITICAL SOCIETY

22

The concept of Law, as the power which holds sway independently of the motives of the individual, has its actualization only in **Political Society**.

23

The **Family** is the *natural* society whose members are united through love, trust and natural obedience (*pietas*).

Explanatory: The Family is a natural society, firstly, because one does not belong to the family through his free act but through nature, and secondly, because the relations and the behaviour of the members of a family toward each other rest not so much upon reflection and deliberate choice but upon feeling and impulse. The relations are necessary and rational but there is lacking the form of conscious deliberation. It is more akin to instinct. The love of the family circle rests upon the fact that each Ego constitutes a unity with the other Egos. They do not regard each other as independent individuals. The family is an organic whole. The parts are, properly speaking, not parts but members which have their substance only in the whole and which lack independence when separated from the whole. The confidence which the different members of the family repose in each other consists in this: that each does not seek his own interest apart from the rest but only the common interest of the whole. The natural obedience within the family rests upon the circumstance that in this whole there is only one will: that, namely, of the head of the family. In so far the family constitutes only *one* person. (Nation)

24

The **State** is human society governed by legal relationships in which all count as persons and not on the basis of particular natural relations which arise from natural inclinations and feelings. The personality of each is respected as a matter of course. If a family has expanded into a nation, and the State and the nation coincide, this is a great good fortune.

Explanatory: A people is knit together by language, manners, customs and culture. This connection, however, is not sufficient to form a State. Besides these the morality, religion, prosperity and wealth of all its citizens are very important things for the State. It must care for the promotion of these conditions but even they do not constitute for it the immediate object of its existence, which is to secure the actualization of Law.

25

The natural condition is the condition of barbarism, of violence and injustice. Man must issue forth from such condition into that of political society because in the latter alone the legal relation has actuality.

Explanatory: The **State of Nature** is frequently depicted as the perfect state of man both as to happiness and ethical development. In the first place it is to be remarked that innocence, as such, has no moral value, in so far as it consists in mere unconsciousness of evil and rests upon the absence of those needs and wants which promote the existence of evil. Secondly, this state of nature is rather one of violence and injustice, for the precise reason that men in this state act towards each other according to their natures. But in this they are unequal, both in regard to bodily power and in mental endowments, and they make these differences felt, one against the other, through brute violence and cunning. Although reason exists in the state of nature it is there subordinate to nature. Man must, therefore, pass over from this state to one in which the rational will has sway.

26

Law is the abstract expression of the Universal Will that exists in-and-for-itself.

Explanatory: Law is the General Will in so far as it accords with Reason. This does not mean that each individual shall have found this will in himself or be conscious of it. Moreover, it is not necessary that each individual shall have declared his will and from this a universal result has been obtained. That is why in actual history it has not happened that each individual citizen of a people has proposed a law and then that all have agreed to it by a common vote. Law contains the necessity of mutual legal relationships. The legislators have not given arbitrary prescriptions. They have prescribed not the product of their particular likes and dislikes but what they have recognized through their incisive minds as the truth and essence of what is just and right.

27

Government is the individuality of Will that is rationally determined. It is the power to make the laws and to administer or execute them.

Explanatory: The State has laws. These are the Will in its general abstract essence which is, as such, inactive; just as principles and maxims express or contain at first only the general nature of the will and not an actual will. To these generalities only the Government is the active and actualizing will. Law has indeed an existence as manners and customs but Government is the conscious power of unconscious custom.

28

The general power of the State contains sundry particular powers subsumed under it:

1. The **Legislative** as such;
2. The **Administrative and Financial**, the power of creating the means for the actualization of its freedom;
3. The [independent] **Judiciary** and **Police** [or the **Public Authority**];
4. The **Military**, and the power to **Wage War** and **Make Peace**.

Explanatory: The form of the constitution is determined principally by the question whether these particular powers are exercised directly by the central government and, moreover, whether several of them are united in one authority or are separated: i.e. whether the prince or regent himself administers the laws or whether particular, special courts are established for this purpose and whether the regency also exercises the ecclesiastical power, etc. It is also an important distinction to note whether in a constitution the highest central power of the government has the financial power in its hands without restriction, so that it can levy taxes and spend them quite arbitrarily and whether several authorities are combined in one, e.g. whether the judicial and the military power are united in one official. The form of a constitution is, furthermore, essentially determined through the circumstance whether or not all citizens, in so far as they are citizens, have a part in the government. Such a constitution as permits this general participation is called a **Democracy**. The degenerate form of a Democracy is called an **Ochlocracy** or mob rule, when, namely, that part of the people who have no property and are not disposed to deal justly prevent, by violent means, the law-abiding citizens from carrying out the business of the State. Only in the case of simple, uncorrupted ethical principles, and in states of small territorial extent, can a Democracy exist and flourish. **Aristocracy** is the constitution in which only certain privileged families have the exclusive right to rule. The degenerate form thereof is an **Oligarchy**, when, namely, the number of families who belong to the governing class is small. Such a condition of affairs is dangerous because in an Oligarchy all particular powers are directly exercised by a council. **Monarchy** is the constitution in which the government is in the hands of one individual and remains hereditary in his family. In a Hereditary Monarchy conflicts and civil wars, such as are liable to happen in an elective kingdom when a change of the occupancy of the throne takes place, vanish because the ambition of powerful individuals cannot, in that case, lead them to aspire to the throne. Moreover, the entire power of the government is not vested immediately in the Monarch but a portion of it is vested in the special Ministries (Bureaus) [and/]or also in the Estates which, in the name of the king and under his supervision and direction, exercise the power entrusted to them by law. In a Monarchy civil freedom is protected to a greater degree than under other constitutions. The degenerate form of a Monarchy is **Despotism**, wherein, namely, the ruler directly governs according to his caprice. It is essential in a Monarchy that the government have appropriate powers to hold in check the private interests of the individual but, on the other hand, the rights of the citizens must be protected by law. A Despotic government has indeed absolute power but in such a constitution the rights of the citizen are sacrificed. The Despot has indeed supreme power and can use the forces of his realm arbitrarily; herein lies the greatest danger. The form of government of a people is not merely an external affair. A people can have one form just as well as another. It depends essentially upon the character, manners and customs, degree of culture, its way of life, and the territorial extent [of the nation].

29

The citizens, as individuals, are subordinated to the power of the State and must obey the same. The content and object of the political power is the actualization of the natural, that is, absolute, rights of the citizens. None of these rights is renounced or given up to the State but they are rather only enjoyed in their full employment and cultivation in the State.

30

The constitution of the State defined as the **Internal Political Law** is the relationship of the particular powers not only to the central administration, their highest unity, but to each other, as well as the relation of the citizens to them or their participation therein.

31

International Law concerns the relation of independent peoples to each other through their governments and rests principally upon special Treaties (*Jus Gentium*).

Explanatory: States are found rather in a natural than in a legal relation towards each other. There is, therefore, a continual state of strife between them until they conclude Treaties with each other and thereby enter into a legal relation towards each other. On the other hand, however, they are quite absolute and independent of each other. The law is, therefore, not actually in force between them. They can, therefore, break treaties in an arbitrary manner and, on this account, there always remains a certain degree of distrust between them. As natural entities they behave towards each other as external forces and, in order to maintain their rights, must, if needs be, wage war for the purpose.

SECOND PART
SCIENCE OF DUTIES OR MORALS

32

Whatever can be demanded on the ground of Law is a **Civil Obligation** [*Schuldigkeit*] but, in so far as moral grounds are to be observed, it is a **Duty** [*Plicht*].

Explanatory: The word Duty is frequently used of legal relationships. Legal Duties are defined as *perfect* and Moral Duties as *imperfect* because the former must be done, and have an external necessity, while the latter depend on a subjective will. But one might, with good reason, invert this classification in as much as the Legal Duty as such demands only an external necessity, in which the disposition is not taken into account, or in which I may even have a bad motive. On the contrary, for a Moral Duty both are demanded, the right deed as regards its content and, likewise according to form, the subjective side, the Good Intention.

33

Law, in general, leaves the disposition out of consideration. Morality, on the other hand, is concerned essentially with the intention and demands that the deed should be done out of simple *regard* [*Achtung*] for Duty. So too the legally right conduct is moral in so far as its moving principle is the regard for the right.

34

The **Disposition** is the subjective side of the moral deed or the *form* of the same. There is in it as yet no content present but the content is as essential as the actual performance.

Explanatory: With legally right conduct the moral aspect should also be essentially connected. It may, however, be the case that with legally right action there is no sentiment of Law present; nay, more, that an immoral intent may accompany it. The legally right act, in so far as it is done out of regard for the Law, is, at the same time, also moral. The legally right action, associated at the same time with a moral disposition, is to be carried out unconditionally before there can be room for the moral action in which there is no legal command, that is, legal obligation. Men are very ready to act from a merely moral ground, for example, to give away with an air of generosity rather than pay their honest debts; for in a generous action they congratulate themselves on account of a special perfection, while, on the contrary, in the performance of just action they would only perform the completely univeral act which makes them equal with all.

Everything Actual contains two aspects: the *true* Concept and the Reality of this Concept: for example, the *concept* of the State is the guarantee and actualization of justice. To the *reality* belong the special regulations of the constitution, the relation of the individual powers to each other, etc. To the *actual* man belong also, even on his practical side, the concept and the reality of the concept. To the former belongs pure personality, or abstract freedom, to the latter, the particular determination of existence and existence itself. Although there is in this something more than is contained in the concept, yet this must also be in conformity to the concept and determined by it. The pure concept of practical existence, the Ego, is the object of Law.

35

Moral action refers to man not as an abstract person but according to the universal and necessary determinations of his *particular determinate existence* [*Daseins*]. The moral code therefore is not merely prohibitory, as with the legal code, which only ordains that the freedom of another must be left inviolate, but it ordains a positive course of action towards another. The prescriptions of Morality refer to individual actuality [i.e. to the concrete situations in which the individual may be placed].

36

Human impulse in respect of man's particular determinate existence as considered by morality is directed towards the harmony of the outer world with his internal determinations, to the production of **Pleasure** and **Happiness**.

Explanatory: Man has impulses, i.e. he has internal determinations in his nature or in that respect according to which he is simply an actual being. These determinations are therefore defective [imperfect] in as much as they are merely internal. They are impulses in so far as they are directed to the overcoming of this defect or want: i.e. they demand their realization, which is the harmony of the outer and inner. This harmony is Pleasure. It is preceded, therefore, by a reflection: a comparison between the inner and the outer, whether this proceeds from me or from good luck. Pleasure may spring from the most varied sources. It does not depend upon the content but concerns only the form. In other words, it is the feeling of something merely formal, namely, of the given harmony. The doctrine which makes Pleasure, or rather Happiness, its aim, has been called **Eudaemonism**. But that doctrine does not decide in what Pleasure or Happiness consists. Hence, there can be a coarse, crude Eudaemonism and a refined one, that is, both good and bad actions can be based on this principle.

37

This harmony is, as Pleasure, a *subjective* feeling and something *contingent*, which can be linked with this or that impulse and its object and in which I regard myself only as a natural being and am an end only as a *single individual*.

Explanatory: Pleasure is something subjective and relates to me as a particular individual. There is in it nothing of an objective, universal, intelligible nature. On this account it is not a standard or rule whereby a thing is to be decided or judged. If I say that a thing pleases me, or if I appeal to my pleasure, I only express the relation of the thing to me and thereby ignore the relation I have to others as a rational being. It is contingent as regards its content because it may attach to this or that object and, since it does not concern the content, it is something purely formal. Moreover, according to its external being, Pleasure is contingent, dependent upon circumstances. The means which I use to attain it are external and do not depend upon me. But the thing that I have obtained through the use of means, in so far as it is to add to my pleasure, must become for me, come to me. But this is a contingent affair. The consequences of what I do, therefore, do not return to me. I have not the enjoyment of them as a necessary consequence. Pleasure thus arises from two different kinds of circumstances: firstly, from an existence which must be sought after and which depends entirely upon good fortune, and secondly, upon a condition of being which I myself produce. Though this condition of things depends, as effect of my action, upon my will, yet only the act as such belongs to me, hence the result does not necessarily return to me and, accordingly, the enjoyment of the act is contingent. In such an act as that of Decius Mus for his native country the effect of the same could not come back to him as enjoyment. Results cannot be made the principle of action. The results of an action are contingent for the reason that they are an externality which depends upon other circumstances or may be annulled altogether.

Pleasure is a secondary affair merely concomitant of an act. When substantial purposes are realized, pleasure accompanies them in so far as one recognizes in his work his own subjective self. Whosoever seeks Pleasure merely seeks his own self according to its accidental side. Whosoever is busied with great works and interests strives only to bring about the realization of the object itself. He directs his attention to the *substantial and does not think of himself but forgets himself in the object*. Men who perform great services, and have charge of great interests, are often commiserated with by people for having little pleasure, that is, for living only in the object and not in their own accidentality.

38

Reason annuls that indeterminateness which feels pleasure in mere objects, purifies the content of our propensities from what is subjective and contingent, and teaches how to recognize what is universal and *essentially the solely desirable* and rather inculcates the disposition to do *worthy actions for their own sake*.

Explanatory: The **Intellect** or **Reflection** transcends in its activity all immediate pleasures but does not, by this, change its aim or guiding principle. It transcends single pleasures only in so far as to compare the impulses one with another and to prefer one over another. Since it aims not at pleasure in detail, but only on the whole, it aims at happiness. This reflection holds fast to the sphere of subjectivity and has pleasure for its end and aim, though in a larger, more comprehensive sense. Since it makes distinctions in pleasures and seeks the agreeable on all its different sides, it refines the grossness, the untamed and merely animal element of pleasure and softens the customs and dispositions. In so far therefore as the understanding busies itself with satisfying the means, the needs generally of gratification, it facilitates this gratification and attains the possibility of devoting itself to higher ends. On the other hand, this refinement of pleasures *weakens* man in as much as he dissipates his powers upon so many things and gives himself so many different aims, and these grow more and more insignificant in so far as their different sides are discriminated. Thus his power is weakened and he becomes less capable of the concentration of his mind wholly upon one object. When man makes pleasure his object he annuls with such a resolution his impulse to transcend pleasure and do something higher.

Pleasure is indefinite in regard to content for the reason that it can be found in the pursuit of all sorts of objects. Therefore, the difference between pleasures is no objective one, but only a *quantitative* one. The Understanding, which takes account of results only, prefers the greater to the less.

Reason, on the contrary, makes a *qualitative* distinction, i.e. a distinction in regard to content. It prefers the worthy object of pleasure to the unworthy one. It therefore enters upon *a comparison of the nature of objects*. In so far it does not regard the subjective as such, i.e. the pleasant feeling, but rather the objective. It teaches, therefore, what kind of objects men should desiderate for themselves. On account of the universality of his nature man has such an infinite variety of sources of pleasure open before him that the path to the agreeable is beset with illusions and he may be easily led astray through this infinite variety itself: i.e. diverted from a purpose which he ought to make his special object.

The urge for what is agreeable may harmonize with Reason, i.e. both may have the same content [and] reason may *legitimate* the content. The form of impulse is that of a subjective feeling or it has for its object the obtaining of what is pleasant for the subject. In dealing with a universal object the object itself is the end and aim. On the other hand the desire for pleasure is always selfish.

39

Impulses and **Inclinations** are, considered by themselves, neither good nor bad; i.e. man has them directly from nature. 'Good' and 'bad' are moral predicates and pertain to the will. The Good is that which corresponds to Reason. But Impulses and Inclinations cannot be considered apart from their relation to the will; this relation is not a contingent one and man is no indifferent twofold being.

Explanatory: Morality has for its object man in his particularity. This seems at first to contain only a multiplicity of peculiarities wherein men are unlike and differ from each other. Men differ from each other in what is contingent or dependent on nature and external circumstances. In the particular, however, there also dwells something universal. The particularity of a man consists in his relation to others. In this relation there are also essential and necessary determinations. These constitute the content of **Duty**.

40

The first essential determination of man is his Individuality; [secondly], he belongs to a natural totality, the Family; [thirdly], he is a member of the State; [fourthly], he stands in relation to Other Men in General.
Consequently his duties are fourfold:

(1) **Duties to Himself**;
(2) **Duties to his Family**;
(3) **Duties to the State**;
(4) **Duties towards Other Men in General**.

Duties of the Individual to Himself

41

Man, as an individual, stands in relation to himself. He has two aspects: his *individuality* and his *universal* essence. His **Duty to Himself** consists partly in his duty to care for his *physical preservation*, partly in his duty to educate himself, to elevate his being as an individual into conformity with his universal nature.
Explanatory: Man is, on the one hand, a natural being. As such he behaves according to caprice and accident as an inconstant, subjective being. He does not distinguish the essential from the unessential. Secondly, he is a spiritual, rational being and as such he is *not by nature what he ought to be*. The animal stands in no need of education, for it is by nature what it ought to be. It is only a natural being. But man has the task of bringing into harmony his two sides, of making his individuality conform to his rational side or of making the latter become his guiding principle. For instance, when man gives way to anger and acts blindly from passion he behaves in an uneducated way because, in this, he takes an injury or affront for something of infinite importance and seeks to make things even by injuring the transgressor in undue measure. It is a lack of education to attach oneself to an interest which does not concern him or in which he cannot accomplish anything through his activity. For it is reasonable to engage one's powers upon such an interest as is within the scope of

one's activity. Moreover, if a man becomes *impatient* under the regular course of events [*Schicksals*] and refuses to submit to the inevitable he elevates his particular interest to a higher degree of importance than his relation to other men and the circumstances warrant.

42

To **Theoretic Education** there belong variety and definiteness of knowledge and the ability to see objects from points of view from which things are to be judged. In addition one should have a sense for objects in their free independence without introducing a subjective interest.

Explanatory: *Variety of knowledge* in-and-for-itself belongs to education for the reason that man, through this, elevates himself above the particular knowledge of insignificant things that surround him to a universal knowledge through which he attains to a greater share in the common stock of information valid for other men and comes into the possession of *universally interesting* objects. When man goes out beyond his immediate knowledge and experience he learns that there are better modes of behaviour and of treating things than his own and that his own are not necessarily the only ones. He separates himself from himself and comes to distinguish the essential from the unessential. *Accuracy of information* relates to essential distinctions, those distinctions which appertain to objects under all circumstances. Education implies the forming of an opinion regarding relations and objects of the actual world. For this it is requisite that one knows what the nature and the purpose of a thing is and what relations it has to other things. These points of view are not immediately gained through sensuous intuition but through attentive study of the thing, through reflection on its purpose and essence, and of whether the means of realizing the same are adequate. The uneducated man remains in the state of simple sensuous intuition, his eyes are not open and he does not see what lies at his very feet. With him it is all subjective seeing and apprehension. He does not see the essential thing. He knows only the nature of things approximately and this never accurately, for it is only the knowledge of general points of view that enables one to decide what is essential. They present the important aspects of things and contain the principal categories under which external existences are classified, and thus the work of apprehending them is rendered easier and more accurate.

The opposite of not knowing how to judge is to make *rash* judgements about everything without understanding them. Such rash judgements are based on partial views, in which one side is seized and the others overlooked, so that the true concept of the thing is missed. An educated man knows at once the *limits of his capacity for judgement*.

Moreover, there belongs to culture the sense for the *objective in its freedom*. It consists in this: that I do not seek my special subjectivity in the object but consider and treat the objects as they are in-and-for-themselves in their free idiosyncrasy: that I interest myself in them without seeking any *gain* for myself. Such an unselfish interest lies in the study of the sciences when one cultivates them for themselves. The desire to make use of natural objects involves the destruction of those objects. The interest for the fine arts is also an unselfish one. Art exhibits things in their living independence and leaves out the imperfect and ill formed and what has suffered from external circumstances. The objective *treatment* consists in this: that it has the *form of the universal* without caprice, whims or arbitrariness and is freed from what is strange or peculiar, etc. and, if one's aim is the genuine *object itself* and not a selfish interest, it must be grasped in the inner essential nature.

43

Practical Education [*Bildung*] entails that man, in the gratification of his natural wants and impulses, shall exhibit that prudence and temperance which lie in the limits of his necessity, namely, self-preservation. He must (a) stand away from and be free from the natural (b) on the other hand, be *absorbed* in his avocation, in what is essential and therefore, (c) be able to confine his gratification of the natural wants not only within the limits of necessity but also to *sacrifice* the same for higher duties.

Explanatory: The freedom of man, as regards natural impulses, consists not in his *being rid* of such impulses altogether and thus striving to escape from his nature but in his recognition of them as a necessity and as something rational; and in realizing them accordingly through his will, he finds himself constrained only in so far as he creates for himself accidental and arbitrary impressions and purposes in opposition to the Universal. The specific, accurate measure, to be followed in the gratification of wants, and in the use of physical and spiritual powers, cannot be accurately given but each can learn for himself what is useful or detrimental to him. **Temperance** in the gratification of natural impulses and in the use of bodily powers is, as such, necessary to *health*. Health is an essential condition for the use of mental powers in fulfilling the higher vocation of man. If the body is not preserved in its proper condition, if it is injured in any one of its functions, then it obliges its possessor to make of it a special object of his care and, by this means, it becomes something dangerous, *absorbing more than its due share of the attention of the mind*. Furthermore, excess in the use or disuse of the physical or mental powers results in *dullness and debility*.

Finally, moderation is closely connected with **Prudence**. The latter consists in reflecting on what one is doing, so that in his enjoyment or work he is not wholly given up to this or that individual state, but remains open to consider something else which may also be necessary. A prudent person distinguishes himself mentally from his condition, his feeling, his occupation. This attitude of not being completely absorbed in one's condition is on the whole requisite in the case of impulses and aims which though necessary are not essential. On the other hand, in the case of a genuine aim or occupation, one's mind must be present in all its earnestness and not at the same time be aloof from it. Hence Prudence consists in being aware of all the details and aspects of the work.

44

As to what concerns one's specific *calling*, which appears as **Fate**, this should not be thought of in the form of an external necessity. It is to be taken up freely, and freely endured and pursued.
Explanatory: With regard to the external circumstances of his lot and all that he *immediately is*, a man must so conduct himself as to make it his own; he must deprive them of the form of external existence. It makes no difference in what external condition man finds himself through good or bad fortune, provided that he is just and right in what he is and does, i.e. that he fulfils all sides of his calling. The **Vocation** of a man, whatever his condition in life may be, is a manifold substance. It is, as it were, a material or stuff which he must elaborate in every direction until it has nothing alien, brittle and refractory within it. In so far as he has made it perfectly his own for himself, he is free therein. A man becomes the prey of discontentment chiefly through the circumstance that he does not fulfil his calling. He enters into a relation which he fails to assimilate thoroughly; at the same time he belongs to this calling: he cannot free himself from it. He lives and acts, therefore, in an adverse relation to himself.

45

To be **Faithful** and **Obedient** in his vocation as well as *submissive* to *his fate* and *self-denying* in his acts, these virtues have their ground in the giving up of vanity, self-conceit, and selfishness in regard to things that are in and for themselves necessary.

Explanatory: The Vocation is something universal and necessary, and constitutes a side of the social life of humanity. It is, therefore, one of the *divisions of human labour*. When a man has a Vocation, he enters into cooperation and participation with the Whole. Through this he becomes objective. The Vocation is a particular, limited sphere, yet it constitutes a necessary part of the whole, and, besides this, is *in-itself a whole*. If a man is *to become something he must know how to limit himself*, that is, make some speciality his Vocation. Then his work ceases to be an irksome restraint to him. He then comes to be at unity with himself, with his externality, with his sphere. He is a universal, a whole. Whenever a man makes something trifling, i.e. unessential or nugatory, his object and aim, then the interest lies not in an object as such, but in it as his object. The trifling object is of no importance by itself, but has importance only to the person who busies himself with it. One sees in a trifling object only oneself; there can be, for example, *a moral vanity*, when a man thinks on the excellence of his acts and is more interested in himself than in the thing. The man who does small things faithfully shows himself capable of greater ones, because he has shown his *obedience*, his self-sacrifice in regard to his own wishes, inclinations and fancies.

46

Through intellectual and moral education a man receives the capacity for *fulfilling duties toward others*, which duties may be called real duties since the duties which relate to his own education are, in comparison, of a more *formal* nature.

47

In so far as the performance of duties appears more as a subjective attribute of the individual, and to pertain chiefly to his natural character, it is properly called **Virtue**.

48

In as much as Virtue in part belongs to the natural character it appears as a peculiar species of morality and of greater vitality and intensity. It is at the same time not so closely connected with the consciousness of duty as is Morality proper.

Duties to the Family

49

When a man is developed by education he has attained a capacity for practical action. In so far as he does act he is necessarily brought into relation to others. The first necessary relation in which the individual stands to others is that of the **Family-relation**. This indeed has a legal side but it is subordinated to the side of moral sentiment, that of love and confidence.

Explanatory: The Family constitutes essentially only *one* substance, only *one* person. The members of the family are not *persons* in their relation to each other. They enter such a relation first when by some calamity the moral bond is destroyed. Among the ancients, the sentiment of family love and action based thereon was called *pietas*. 'Piety' has with us the sense of devoutness or godliness, which it has in common with the ancient meaning of the word in that both presuppose an *absolute* bond, the self-existent unity in a spiritual substance, a bond which is not formed through particular caprice or accident.

50

This sentiment, precisely stated, consists in this: that each member of the Family has his essence not in his own person, but that only the whole of the Family constitutes his personality.

51

The union of persons of opposite sex which **Marriage** is, is not merely a *natural*, animal union, nor, at the other extreme, is it a mere *civil contract*, rather it is essentially a moral union of sentiment [*Gesinnung*] in reciprocal love and confidence which constitutes them *one* person.

52

The duty of *parents towards children* is to care for their *support* and education; that of the *children* to *obey* their parents until they grow up and become independent and to *honour and respect* them through life; that of brothers and sisters, to treat each other with the utmost consideration.

Duties to the State

53

The natural whole, which constitutes the family, expands into a whole of a **People** and a **State** in which the individuals have for themselves an independent will.
Explanatory: The State, in one respect, is able to dispense with the goodwill and consent of citizens, i.e. in so far as it must be independent of the will of the individual. It prescribes, therefore, to the individual his obligations, namely, the part which he must perform for the whole. It cannot leave this to his goodwill because he may be self-interested and oppose himself to the interest of the State. In this way the State becomes a *machine*, a system of external dependencies. But, on the other hand, it cannot dispense with the [*good*] *disposition* of its citizens. The order issued by the government can contain only what is general. The actual deed, the fulfilment of the State's aim, requires a special form of activity. This can come only from individual intelligence and from the goodwill and consent of men.

54

The State holds society not only under legal relations but mediated as a true, higher, moral commonwealth, the union in customs, education and general form of thinking and acting, since each one views and recognizes in the other his universality in a spiritual manner.

55

In the **Spirit of a People** each individual citizen has his spiritual substance. Not only does the preservation of the individual depend on the preservation of this living whole, but this living whole *is* the universal spiritual nature or the essence of each one as opposed to his individuality. *The preservation of the whole takes precedence, therefore, over the preservation of the individual* and all citizens should act on this conviction.

56

Considered according to the merely legal side, in so far as the State protects the private rights of the individual and the individual looks after his own rights, there is indeed possible a sacrifice of a part of his property for the preservation of the rest. **Patriotism**, however, is not founded on this calculation, but on the consciousness of the *absoluteness of the State*. This disposition to offer up property and life for the whole is the greater in a people the more the individuals can act for the whole from their *own will* and self-activity and the greater the confidence they have in the whole. (Speak here of the beautiful patriotism of the Greeks; also of the distinction between *bourgeois* and *citoyen*.)

57

The disposition *to obey* the commands of the government, attachment to princes and the constitutional form of government, the feeling of *national honour*, all these are virtues of the citizen in every well-ordered State.

58

The State rests not upon an express contract of one with all or of all with one or between the individual and the government. The Universal Will of the whole is not simply the expressed will of the individual but is the Absolute Universal Will which is in-and-for-itself binding on the individual.

Duties toward Others

59

The duties toward others are, first, the legal duties which must be linked with the disposition to do the lawful for the sake of Law. The rest of these duties are founded on the disposition to regard others not merely as abstract persons but also, in their particularity, as possessing equal rights and to regard their welfare or bad fortune as one's own concern and to manifest this feeling by active help.

60

This moral mode of thinking and acting goes further than is demanded by the mere legal right. But **Integrity**, the observance of the strict duties toward others, is the first duty and lies at the basis of all others. There may be noble and generous actions which lack integrity. In that case they have their ground in self-love and in the consciousness of having done something special, whereas that which integrity demands is valid for all and is no arbitrary duty.

61

Among the special duties to others, the first is **Truthfulness** in speech and action. It consists in the identity of that which is and of which one is conscious, with what he expresses and shows to others.

Untruthfulness is the disagreement and contradiction between what one is in his own consciousness and what he is for others, hence between his inner being and his actuality, and is therefore a nullity in itself.

62

It is especially untruthful when what one imagines to be a good intention or disposition is in fact bad and harmful. (This disagreement between the disposition and the action could at least be called clumsiness but, in so far as the doer is responsible, if he does what is bad he must be regarded as also meaning his action to be bad.)

63

It implies the existence of a special relation between individuals to give one of them the right to speak truthfully regarding the other's behaviour. When one undertakes to do this without the right he is himself, in so far, untrue, since he assumes a relation to another which has no existence.

Explanatory: It is of the first importance to *speak the truth* in so far as one knows that it is the truth. It is mean not to speak the truth when it is one's duty to speak it, because thereby one is demeaned in one's own eyes and in the eyes of the other. But also one should not speak the truth where he is not called upon to do so or does not even have the right to do so. When one speaks the truth merely for the sake of having his say and without following it up, this is at least *superfluous*, for what is important is not that I have spoken but that the matter in hand should be achieved. Speaking is not yet the deed or act; the latter is superior. The truth then is spoken in the right place at the right time when it serves to bring about the matter in hand. Speech is an astonishingly great means but to use it correctly demands great understanding.

64

Malicious Gossip is akin to **Slander** which is an actual lie. The former is the retailing of matters which compromise the honour of a third party and which are not absolutely evident to the narrator. It usually happens out of a zealous disapproval of immoral actions, usually with the comment that the narrator cannot vouch for the truth of the stories and wishes he had not said anything about them, but in this case there is associated the *dishonesty* of alleging that he does not want to spread the stories and yet by his action actually does so. He is guilty of *hypocrisy* in pretending to speak in the interest of

morality and at the same time behaving badly.
Explanatory: **Hypocrisy** consists in behaving badly while assuming the appearance of having a good intention, of wanting to do something good. The external deed is, however, not different from the internal one. In the case of a bad deed the intention was also essentially bad and not good. It may be the case that a man has accomplished something good or at least not improper but it is not permissible to make of that which is in its own self evil a means with which to achieve a good end. The *end* or the *intention does not sanctify the means*. Moral principle concerns chiefly the disposition or the intention. It is, however, just as essential that not only the intention but *also the action be good*. Moreover, a man must not persuade himself that he has excellent and important purposes in the common acts of his individual life. In that case it frequently happens that while he bases his own deeds on good intentions and seeks to make his unimportant deeds great by his reflections he is apt, on the other hand, to attribute a selfish or bad motive to the great or at least good deeds of others.

65

The disposition to injure others, knowingly and willingly, is Evil. The disposition which permits itself to violate duties to others and also to itself, and from weakness to resist its inclinations, is Bad.
Explanatory: **Good** stands opposed to **Evil** [*böse*] as also to **Bad** [*schlecht*]. To be Evil involves an act of the will; it presupposes a *strength of will* which is also a condition of the Good, but the Bad, on the contrary, is something devoid of will. The Bad individual follows his inclinations and neglects duties. It would be perfectly satisfactory to him to fulfil the duties if he could do so without effort but he has not the will to master his inclinations or habits.

66

The **Services** we are able to perform for others depend upon the contingent relations in which we happen to stand with them and upon the special circumstances in which we are situated. When we are in a position to do another a Service we have only to consider two things: that he is a *human being* and has a *need*.
Explanatory: The first condition precedent to rendering help to others consists in this: that we have a right to regard them as in need and to act toward them as sufferers. Help must not be given, therefore, *without their willingness* to receive it. This presupposes a certain degree of acquaintance or confidence. The needy are as such not on the same

footing as regards equality with those not in need. It is a matter for him to decide whether or not he wants to *appear as one in need*. He consents to this when he is convinced that I regard him as my equal, and treat him as such in spite of this inequality of condition. In the second place, I must have in hand the means with which to help him. Finally, there may happen cases where his want is of so evident a character as to render unnecessary an express consent on his part to receive assistance.

67

The duty of the **Universal Love of Humanity** also includes those cases wherein we love those with whom we stand in relations of acquaintance and friendship. The original unity of mankind must be the basis from which arise voluntarily, much closer, connections as involve more particular duties. (**Friendship** rests on likeness of character and especially of interest, engagement in a common work, rather than in liking for the person of another as such. One should cause his friends as little trouble as possible. To require no services of friends is the most delicate way. One should spare no pains to avoid laying others under obligations to him.)

68

The duty of **Prudence** [Policy] appears, at first, in so far as the end is a selfish one, as a duty toward oneself in his relations to others. True selfishness is, however, essentially attained through moral conduct and this, consequently, is the true Prudence. It is a principle of moral conduct that private gain may be a result but must never constitute the motive.

69

In as much as private gain does not constitute the direct result of moral conduct but depends rather upon the particular and, on the whole, accidental goodwill of others, there is to be found the sphere of mere inclination or favour, but Prudence consists in this: that one does not interfere with the inclinations of others but acts in their interest. But also, in this respect, that which proves politic is really that which recommends itself for its own sake, namely, to leave others free where we have neither duty nor right to disturb them and, through our correct conduct, to win their favour.

70

Courtesy [Politeness] is the mark of a well-wishing disposition and also of a readiness to do a service to others, especially to those with whom we stand in a nearer relation of acquaintance or friendship. It is false when it is connected with the opposite disposition. True Courtesy is, however, to be regarded as a duty because we ought to have benevolent intentions toward each other in general in order to open by means of polite actions the way to closer union. To do a service, an act of politeness, something pleasant to a stranger, is Courtesy. The same thing should, however, be done to an acquaintance or friend. Toward strangers and those with whom we stand in no nearer relations there is the appearance of goodwill and this is all that is required. **Refinement** and **Delicacy** consist in doing or saying no more than is allowed by the relation in which one stands to other parties. (Greek Humanity and Urbanity in the time of Socrates and Plato)

THIRD PART
THE SCIENCE OF RELIGION

71

The **Moral Law** within us is the **Eternal Law of Reason** which we must respect without reserve and by which we must feel indissolubly bound. We see, however, the immediate *incommensurateness* of our individuality with it and recognize it as higher than ourselves, as a Being independent from us, self-existent and absolute.

72

This Absolute Being is present in our pure consciousness and reveals Himself to us therein. The knowing of Him is, as mediated through our pure consciousness, for us immediate and called **Faith**.

73

The elevation above the sensuous and finite constitutes in a negative form the mediation of this knowing, but only in so far as having originated from a sensuous and finite. The latter is at the same time abandoned and recognized in its nullity. But this *knowing of the Absolute* is itself an *absolute* and immediate knowing and cannot have anything finite as its positive ground or be mediated through anything that is not itself a proof.

74

This knowing must determine itself more closely and not remain a mere inner feeling, a faith in an undefined Being in general, but become a cognition of it. The cognition of God is not above Reason, for Reason is only God's image and reflection and is essentially the knowledge of the Absolute. But such cognition is above the Understanding, the knowledge of what is finite and relative.

75

Religion itself consists in the employment or exercise of feeling and thought in forming an idea or representation of the Absolute Being, wherewith is necessarily connected *forgetfulness* of one's own particularity and actions from this disposition [*Sinn*] in regard to the absolute Being.

76

God is the **Absolute Spirit**, i.e. he is the pure Being that makes himself his own object and in this contemplates only himself, or who is, in his other-being, absolutely returned into himself and self-identical.

77

God is, according to the moments of his Being: (1) **Absolutely Holy**, in as much as he is in himself the purely universal Being; (2) **Absolute Power**, in as much as he actualizes the universal and preserves the individual in the universal or is the Eternal Creator of the Universe; (3) **Wisdom**, in so far as his power is only holy power; (4) **Goodness**, in so far as he allows the individual in his actual existence to be a free agent; and (5) **Justice**, in so far as he eternally brings the individual back to the universal.

78

Evil is alienation from God in so far as the individual, in his freedom, separates himself from the universal and strives by excluding himself from it to become absolute for himself. In so far as it is the nature of the finite free being to reflect itself into this individuality, this nature is to be regarded as Evil.

79

But the freedom of the individual being is at the same time implicitly, or in-itself, an identity of the divine Being with himself or it is, in-itself, of divine nature. This knowledge, that human nature is not truly alien to the divine nature, is assured to man by **Divine Grace**; which Grace allows him to lay hold of this knowledge whereby through it the *reconciliation* of God with the world is achieved or man's alienation from God disappears.

80

The **Divine Service** is the specific occupation of the thought and feelings with God whereby the individual strives to bring about his union with God and to become conscious and assured of this union. The harmony of his will with the divine will should be demonstrated by the spirit in which he acts in his daily life.

2
PHENOMENOLOGY
[For the Middle Class]

INTRODUCTION

[1]
Our ordinary **Knowing** has before itself only the *object* which it knows, but does not at the same time make an object of itself, i.e. of the Knowing. But the whole which is present in the act of knowing is not the object alone but also the 'I' [Ego] that knows and the relation of the Ego and the object to each other, i.e. Consciousness.

2
In Philosophy the determinations of Knowing are not considered one-sidedly only as determinations of things but as, at the same time, determinations of the Knowing to which they belong in common at least with the things. In other words they are not taken merely as *objective* but also as *subjective* determinations or rather as specific kinds of the relation of the object and subject to each other.

3
Since things and their determinations *are* in the Knowing it is possible, on the one hand, to think of them as in-and-for-themselves outside of Consciousness, as given to the latter in the shape of alien and already existing material for it. On the other hand, since Consciousness is equally essential to the Knowing of these [material things] it is also possible to think that Consciousness itself posits this, its world, and produces or modifies, either wholly or in part, the determinations of the same through its behaviour and its activity. The former point of view is called **Realism** the latter **Idealism**. Here we are to consider the universal determinations of things simply as the specific relation of the object to the subject.

4

The subject, thought of more specifically, is Mind [or Spirit]. It is *phenomenal [erscheinend]* when essentially relating to an existent object: i.e. in so far it is Consciousness. The Science of Consciousness is, therefore, called **The Phenomenology of Mind** [or **Spirit**].

5

But Mind as spontaneously active within itself and as self-referential [*Beziehung auf sich*] and independent of all reference to others is considered in the Doctrine of Mind or **Psychology**.

6

Consciousness is, in general, the knowing of an object, whether external or internal, without regard to whether it presents itself without the help of Mind or whether it be produced by it. Mind is to be considered in its activities in so far as the determinations of its Consciousness are ascribed to itself.

7

Consciousness is the specific relation of the Ego to an object. In so far as one starts from the object, consciousness can be said to vary according to the *diversity of the objects* which it has.

8

At the same time, however, the object is essentially determined in its relation to Consciousness. Its diversity is, therefore, to be considered conversely as dependent upon the *further development* of Consciousness. This *reciprocity* proceeds in the phenomenal sphere of Consciousness itself and leaves the matters in paragraph 3 above undecided.

9

Consciousness has, in general, three stages [*Stufen*] according to the diversity of the object. It [the object] is namely [a] either the object standing opposed to the Ego or [b] the Ego itself or [c] something objective which belongs likewise equally to the Ego, [e.g.] Thought. These determinations are not empirically taken up from without but are moments of Consciousness itself. Hence Consciousness is:

(1) **Consciousness in General**;
(2) **Self-Consciousness**;
(3) **Reason**.

FIRST STAGE
CONSCIOUSNESS IN GENERAL

10

Consciousness in General is:
(a) **Sensuous**;
(b) **Perceiving**;
(c) **Understanding**.

The Sensuous Consciousness

11

The simple **Sensuous Consciousness** is the immediate certainty of an external object. The expression for the immediacy of such an object is that it *is*, and indeed is *this* object, a **Now** according to time and a **Here** according to space, [and is] completely different from all other objects and completely determined in-itself.

12

Both this Now and this Here are vanishing determinatenesses. Now is no more even while it is and another Now has taken its place, and this latter Now has likewise immediately vanished. But the Now abides all the same. This abiding Now is the universal Now which is both this and the other Now, and also neither of them. This Here which I mean, and point out has a right and left, an above and a below, a behind and a before, etc. *ad infinitum*, i.e. the Here pointed out, is not a simple and hence specific Here but a totality of many Heres. Therefore what in truth is before us is not the abstract, sensuous determinateness but the universal.

Perception

13

Perception has no longer for [its] object the sensuous in so far as it is immediate but, in so far as it is also universal, it is a mingling of sensuous determinations with those of Reflection.

14

The object of this Consciousness is, therefore, the **Thing** with its **Properties**. The sensuous properties (a) are for-themselves not only immediately in Feeling but also at the same time determined through the relation to others and mediated; (b) *belong to a Thing* and, in this respect, on the one hand are included in the *individuality* of the same,

[and] on the other hand have *universality* in accordance with which they transcend this individual thing and are at the same time independent of one another.

15

In so far as **Properties** are essentially mediated they have their subsistence in an Other and are *alterable*. They are only **Accidents**. Things, however, since they subsist in their properties, for the reason that they are distinguished by means of these, perish through the alteration of those properties and are an alternation of *coming-to-be* and *ceasing-to-be*.

16

In this alternation it is not merely the something that sublates itself and becomes an Other but the Other also ceases to be. But the Other of the Other, or the alteration of the alterable, is the *Becoming of the enduring* [*Werden des Bleibenden*], of that which subsists in-and-for-itself and is inner.

The Understanding

17

The object has now this determination: it has (a) a purely accidental side but (b) also an essential and permanent side. Consciousness, in that the object has for it this character, is the **Understanding** in which the the Things of perception pass for mere *phenomena* and it [the Understanding] contemplates the **Inner** of Things.

18

On the one hand, the Inner of Things is that in them which is free from their appearances, namely, their **Manifoldness** which constitutes an outer in opposition to the inner, [and] on the other hand, however, the inner is that which is related to them through its concept. It is therefore:
(1) simple **Force**, which passes over in Determinate Being into its **Expression** [or Manifestation].

19

(2) **Force** remains with this difference the same in all the sensuous variety of Appearance. The *law* of Appearance is its quiescent, universal image. It is a relation of universal abiding determinations whose distinctions are external to the law. The universality and persistence of this relation does indeed lead to its necessity but

without the difference being one determined in-and-for-itself or inner, in which one of the determinations lies immediately in the concept of the other.

20

This concept, applied to Consciousness itself, gives another stage thereof. Hitherto it was in relation to its object as something alien and indifferent. Since now the difference in general has become a difference which at the same time is no difference, the previous mode of the difference of Consciousness from its object falls away. It has an object and is related to an Other, which, however, is at the same time no 'Other'; *in fine*, it has itself for object.

21

In other words, the Inner of Things is the **Thought** or Concept of them. While Consciousness has the Inner as object it has Thought or equally its own Reflection or Form and, [consequently], simply has itself for object.

SECOND STAGE
SELF-CONSCIOUSNESS

22

As **Self-Consciousness** the Ego intuits itself, and the expression of this in its purity is Ego = Ego, or: I am I.

23

This proposition of Self-Consciousness is devoid of all content. The urge of Self-Consciousness consists in this: to realize its concept and in everything to become conscious of itself. It is, therefore, active (a) in overcoming the *otherness* of objects and in positing them as the same as itself [and] (b) in externalizing itself and thereby giving itself objectivity and determinate being. These two are one and the same activity. Self-Consciousness in becoming determined is at the same time a self-determining and, conversely, it produces itself as object.

24

Self-Consciousness has, in its formative development or movement, three stages:
(1) Of **Desire** in so far as it is directed to other things;
(2) Of the relation of **Master and Slave** in so far as it is directed to

another Self-Consciousness unlike itself;
(3) Of the **Universal Self-Consciousness** which recognizes itself in other Self-Consciousnesses and is identical with them as they are identical with it.

Desire

25

Both sides of Self-Consciousness, the positing and the sublating, are thus united with each other immediately. Self-Consciousness posits itself through negation of otherness and is *practical* Consciousness. If, therefore, in Consciousness proper, which also is called *theoretical* [Consciousness], the determinations of it and of the object altered themselves in-themselves, this now happens through the activity of Consciousness itself and *for* it. It is aware that this sublating activity belongs to it. In the concept of Self-Consciousness lies the determination of the as yet unrealized difference. In so far as this difference does make its appearance in it there arises a feeling of an *otherness* in consciousness itself, a feeling of a negation of itself or the feeling of a lack, a need.

26

This feeling of its otherness contradicts its identity with itself. The felt necessity to overcome this opposition is **Impulse, Negation** or **Otherness**, [and] presents itself to consciousness as an external thing different from it, but which is determined by Self-Consciousness, (a) as a something suited to gratify the Impulse and (b) as something in-itself negative whose subsistence is to be sublated by the Self and posited in identity with it.

27

The activity of **Desire** thus overcomes the *otherness* of the object and its subsistence and unites it with the subject, whereupon the Desire is satisfied. This is accordingly conditioned, (a) by an object existing externally or indifferent to it, or through Consciousness; and (b) by its activity producing the gratification only through overcoming the object. Self-Consciousness comes therefore only to its feeling of Self.

28

In Desire, Consciousness stands in relation to itself as an individual. It is related to a selfless object which is, in-and-for-itself, an other than the Self-Consciousness. The latter therefore only attains self-identity as regards the object by overcoming the latter. Desire is in general destructive [and], in its gratification therefore, it only gets as far as the self-feeling of the subject's being-for-self as an individual: [i.e.] to the indeterminate concept of the subject in its connection with objectivity.

The Relation of Master and Slave

29

The concept of Self-Consciousness as a Subject which is at the same time objective, yields the relation that *another* Self-Consciousness exists for Self-Consciousness.

30

A Self-Consciousness which is for another is not for it a mere object but is its other self. The Ego is no abstract universality in which, as such, there is no distinction or determination. Since Ego is, therefore, object for the Ego the object is, in this relation, the same as that which the Ego is. It beholds in the other its own self.

31

This beholding of oneself in another is the abstract moment of self-sameness. But each has also the determination of appearing to the other as an external object and, in so far, as an immediate, sensuous and *concrete* existence. Each exists absolutely for-itself as an individual opposed to the other and demands to be regarded and treated as such by the other and to behold in the other its own freedom as an independent being or to be *acknowledged* by it.

32

In order to make itself valid as a free being and to obtain recognition, Self-Consciousness must exhibit itself to another as free from natural existence. This moment is as necessary as that of the freedom of Self-Consciousness within itself. The absolute identity of the Ego with itself is essentially not an immediate identity but one which has been achieved by overcoming sensuous immediacy and, by so doing, has also made itself free and independent of the sensuous for another. It thus shows itself to conform to its concept and must be recognized because it gives reality to the Ego.

33

But independence is freedom not so much *outside of* and [*apart*] *from* sensuous immediate existence, as rather a freedom *in* it. The one moment is as necessary as the other but they are not of the same value, since inequality enters, namely, that to one of the two Self-Consciousness[es] freedom passes for the essential in opposition to sensuous existence, while with the other the opposite occurs. With the reciprocal demand for recognition there enters into determinate actuality the relation of master and slave between them or, in general terms, that of service and obedience, so far as this diversity of independence is present through the immediate agency of nature.

34

Since of the two Self-Consciousness[es] opposed to each other each must strive to prove and maintain itself as an absolute being-for-self against and for the other, that one enters into a condition of Slavery who prefers life to freedom and thereby shows that he is incapable of making abstraction from his sensuous existence by his own efforts in order to achieve his independence.

35

This purely negative freedom, which consists in the abstraction from natural existence, does not, however, correspond to the concept of Freedom, for this latter is self-sameness in otherness, that is, in part the beholding of oneself in another self and in part freedom not *from* existence but *in* existence, a freedom which itself has an existence. The one who serves lacks a self and has another self in place of his own; so that in the Master he has alienated and annulled himself as an individual Ego and now views another as his essential self. The Master, on the contrary, sees in the Servant the other Ego as annulled and his own individual will as preserved. (History of Robinson Crusoe and Friday.)

36

The Servant's own individual will, considered more closely, is suppressed in the fear of the Master, in the inner feeling of its own negativity. Its labour for the service of another is an alienation of its own will, partly in principle, partly at the same time, with the negation of its own desire, the positive transformation of external things through labour; since through labour the self makes its own determinations into the forms of things and in its work views itself as an objective self. The renunciation of the unessential arbitrary will constitutes the moment of true obedience. (Pisistratus taught the Athenians to obey. Through this he made the Code of Solon an actual power and, after the Athenians had learned this, the dominion of a Ruler over them was superfluous.)

37

This renunciation of Individuality as Self is the moment by which Self-Consciousness makes the transition to being the Universal Will: [i.e.] the transition to Positive Freedom.

Universality of Self-Consciousness

38

The **Universal Self-Consciousness** is the intuition of itself not as a particular existence distinct from others but as the implicit universal self. Thus it recognizes itself and the other Self-Consciousnesses within it and is, in turn, recognized by them.

39

Self-Consciousness is, according to this its essential universality, only real to itself in so far as it knows its reflection in others. (I know that others know me as themselves.) And as pure spiritual universality, as belonging to the family, one's native land, etc., [it] knows itself as an essential self. This Self-Consciousness is the basis of every virtue, of love, honour, friendship, bravery, all self-sacrifice, all fame, etc.

THIRD STAGE
REASON

40

Reason is the highest union of consciousness and self-consciousness or of the knowing of an object and of the knowing of itself. It is the certainty that its determinations are just as much objective, i.e. determinations of the essence of things, as they are our own thoughts. It is equally the certainty of itself, subjectivity, as being or objectivity in one and the same thinking activity.

41

Or what we see through the insight of Reason is (a) a content which does not consist in our mere subjective ideas or thoughts which we make for ourselves but which contains the absolute essence of objects and possesses objective reality, and (b) a content which is, for the Ego, nothing alien, nothing given from without but is throughout penetrated and assimilated by the Ego and therefore, to all intents, produced by the Ego.

42

The knowing of Reason is therefore not mere subjective certainty but also **Truth**, because Truth consists in the agreement, or rather *unity*, of certainty and being or of certainty and objectivity.

3
LOGIC
[For the Lower Class]

1
A **Sensation** is the mode in which we are affected by an external object [*Gegenstand*].

2
A **Representation**, generally, is this determination, in so far as it is attributed to the object, a determination which the object has whether we are affected by it or not.

[3]
A **Sensuous Representation** is the determination which an object has in so far as we relate it only through the senses, or immediately.

[4]
Intellectual Representation.

LOGIC

1
Philosophy is the science of the absolute ground of things, that is, their ground not in their Individuality or Particularity but in their Universality.

2
Thinking considers the Universal of things. Logic is the Science of such Thinking.

3
Sensation is the mode in which, and in so far as, we are affected by an object.

4

In **Representative Thinking** [*Vorstellen*] we separate ourselves from the object and attribute to it the determinations which it has, without regard to whether we are affected by them or not.

[5]

A sensuous external object is directly perceived by us and is a single object of various sensuous determinations or properties which belong to Sensation and which become something objective in Representation.

[6]

A determination of this kind taken by itself and separated from the others with which it was connected in the object is an **Abstract Sensuous Representation**.

[7]

A determination of this kind does not belong to any single object but to several or is common to them and therefore a **Universal Sensuous Representation**.

[8]

At the same time it is no longer wholly immediate, as it was in Sensation, but is also a mediated determination since it has originated through being separated from the other determinations and from the single object.

[9]

One side of the determination belongs to Sensation, namely Sensuous Individuality. But it also has a side which is constituted by Sensuous Universality and is the form of Sensuousness. This form is the dual one of space and time.

[10]

The two are inseparable continua in which the differences and limitations posited in them do not constitute a genuine limit but only a quantitative one.

[11]

Space is the connection of the quiescent asunderness and side-by-sideness of things; **Time** is the connection of their vanishing or alteration.

[12]

The external object contains further determinations which belong to the intellect and are universal non-sensuous forms and are called **Categories**.

[13]

Above the Category again stands the **Concept** which is not only a universal thought determination but which expresses the specific nature of an object and together with Judgements and Syllogisms is treated in the ordinary so-called Logic. It is divided into:
[1] **The Doctrine of Concepts**,
[2] **[The Doctrine of] Judgements** and
[3] **[The Doctrine of] Syllogisms**.

THE DOCTRINE OF THE CONCEPT

[14]

The **Concept** does not contain the manifold and sensuous determinations of an external object but those which accord (a) with its Universal Essence and (b) with its Essential Particularity. The Determinate Being of the Concept constitutes the moment of Individuality.

[15]

The **Universal Essence** and the **Particularity** of an object, by which it is distinguished from others and which is a limitation of the Universal, belong to the conceptual characteristics of an external object.

[16]

The Universal is restricted in Particularity without thereby suffering an alteration; the case is similar with the restriction of the Particular by the Universal; though, conversely, the Individual that is expanded to the Particular is expanded to the Universal.

[17]

The Universal *includes* the Particular and the Individual and the Particular *includes* the Individual. The Particular and the Individual are *subsumed* under the Universal and the Individual under the Particular. What holds good of the Universal also holds good of the Particular and the Individual and what holds good of the Particular also holds good of the Individual but the converse is not true.

FACULTY OF JUDGEMENT

[18]

Judgement is the relation to one another of two determinations of the Concept, one of which is related as Individual to the other as Particular or Universal or is related as Particular to the Universal.

[19]

Of two determinations related to one another, the less inclusive narrower one is the **Subject**, the other is the **Predicate**, and the connection between them, the 'is', is the **Copula**.

[20]

Logic abstracts from all empirical content and considers only that content which is posited by the form of the relation itself; accordingly the Logical Judgement means, strictly, that an Individual is a Particular or a Universal or that the Particular is a Universal.

[21]

Not every proposition is a Judgement but rather only in so far as its content has that relationship.

[22]

Furthermore, since in the Judgement the determinations of the Concept fall apart, only that proposition is a Judgement in which the Predicate is presented on its own account and is connected with the Subject by comparison.

[23]

The Predicate of the Judgement considered more closely (a) is simply a determination relating to the Subject or to other determinations and has from this side a content, (b) is unequal to the Subject, as Universal in relation to the Individual as (c) connected with the Subject; it is restricted to it and can be regarded as only of the same scope as that of the Subject.

[24]

The Subject (a) is likewise distinct from other Subjects, (b) is likewise distinct from the Predicate as one that is subsumed under it, (c) is equal to the Predicate which expresses its content so that, strictly, in the Judgement nothing is expressed of the Subject other than what is contained in the Predicate.

A *Judgement of Inherence or Quality*

[25]

The Predicate in the Judgement is in the first place a quality, any simple immediate determinateness or property which inheres in the Subject, several of which the Subject contains within itself.

[26]

Since in the **Qualitative Judgement** the Predicate is affirmed of the Subject it is a **Positive Judgement**.

[27]

The principle is of wider scope than the Subject. If, therefore, the Positive Judgement were immediately converted, i.e. the Predicate were made the Subject and the Subject the Predicate, the Predicate would then be more restricted than the Subject, which is contrary to the Concept of the Judgement.

[28]

Consequently a Positive Judgement can only be converted in so far as the Predicate is expressed as taken in its restriction to the Subject.

[29]

A **Negative Judgement** is one in which a Predicate of a Subject is simply negated.

[30]

The Predicate, considered more closely, has in it two moments: that of the determinateness in relation to others and that of the Universal sphere. In the Negative Judgement only the Predicate as a determinateness is negated but not the Universal sphere of the Predicate.

[31]

Or, in the Negative Judgement the Subject is negatively related to the Predicate. With negation therefore there is, at the same time, present a positing of the Predicate and that too of the Predicate as a Universal sphere.

[32]

A Negative Judgement can be converted directly.

[33]

An **Infinite Judgement** is one in which not only the determinateness of the Predicate but also the Universal sphere is negated.

[34]

The Infinite Judgement includes the further meaning that what a Subject is is not exhausted in a Predicate which expresses one of its qualities, or in so far as this quality expresses a closely related determinateness, still less in so far as it contains a further determinateness which belongs to the Universal sphere.

B *Judgements of Quantity or Reflection*

[35]

To **Reflect** means to move on beyond something and to grasp the resultant unity.

[36]

A determinateness of reflection contains, therefore, partly a comparison with something else and the side according to which the object in its qualities is similar to or different from it, partly a grasp of its own determinations, a grasp which, however, expresses only an external Universality and common nature or only a mere completeness.

[37]

The **Individual Judgement** expresses that Predicate of a Subject which belongs to it alone or whereby the Subject is distinguished from all others; the Subject is in so far, likewise, an Individual.

[38]

An Individual Judgement can, in a wider sense, also be called such when its Subject is an Individual even though a Universal Predicate is asserted of it, but which at least serves to distinguish it from others which come into consideration.

[39]

A **Particular Judgement** has for its Subject several Individuals. In the Universal Judgement the Subject is a taking together of all the Individuals of a kind; this taking together is the 'allness' or Universality of reflection; the Predicate belonging to such a Subject is likewise the Universal of these Individuals, namely, as their common element.

C *Judgements of Relation or Necessity*

[40]

Subject and Predicate of necessity [belong] together through their content.

[41]

Categorical Judgements: the Predicate expresses the nature or the genuine Universal of the Subject and both have the same essential content and the Subject is only a Particularity of the Predicate. The further determination[s] which the Subject still has besides what such a Predicate contains are unessential properties or only limitations of them.

[42]

In the **Hypothetical Judgement** the necessity does not lie in the sameness of the content which rather is different, and what is declared in this Judgement is only that two determinations stand in a necessary connection as ground and consequent.

[43]

In the **Disjunctive Judgement** the Subject is considered as a Universal sphere which in so far could have various determinations but, because these mutually exclude one another, must necessarily have only one of them excluding the others.

D *Modality [of Judgement]*

[44]

To consider Judgements according to their **Modality** means to inquire whether the Predicate expresses the appropriateness of the determinate being of the Subject to the Concept.

[45]

In **Assertoric Judgements** the specific nature of the Subject is not yet developed.

[46]

Against the mere undeveloped, unfounded assurance of the assertoric Judgement the opposite assurance can be asserted with the same formal right. The Consequence in that which is present is only the possibility that one Predicate, or its opposite, belongs to the Subject. Thus the Judgement is **Problematic**.

[47]

The Subject is, therefore, to be posited with a determination which expresses its specific nature, in which lies the appropriateness or inappropriateness of the existence with the Concept. This Judgement is **Apodictic**.

SYLLOGISM

[48]

In the Judgement two moments of the Concept are directly connected with each other; the **Syllogism** contains their mediation or ground. In it two determinations are linked together by a third which is their unity.

[49]

The two linked determinations are the **Extremes** (*termini extremi*); the determination linking them is their **Middle Term** (*terminus medius*).

[50]

The Middle Term subsumes Individuality and is subsumed under Universality.

[51]

Since the Universal subsumes under it the Particular, but the Particular subsumes under it the Individual, so too does the Universal subsume under it the Individual and the former is the Predicate of the latter. Or, conversely, since the Individual contains within itself the determination of the Particular but the Particular contains within itself the determination of the Universal, the Individual thus also contains within itself the Universal.

[52]

The connections of the Extremes to the Middle Term are direct; these connections expressed as propositions or Judgements are called **Premisses of the Syllogism**, that which contains the Extreme of Universality (*terminus major*), the major proposition, that which contains the Extreme of Individuality, the minor proposition.

[53]

The connection of the two Extremes is mediated and is called the **Conclusion** (*conclusio*).

[54]
The minor premiss cannot be negative.
 Proposition not Particular.
 The *medius terminus* in the major premiss [is] not Particular.

LOGIC
[For the Middle Class]

INTRODUCTION

1

The **Science of Logic** has for its object the Thinking Activity and the entire compass of its determinations. 'Natural Logic' is a name given to the natural understanding which man possesses by nature and the immediate use which he makes of it. The Science of Logic, however, is the Knowing of Thinking in its truth.

Explanatory: Logic considers the province of **Thought** in general. Thinking is its peculiar sphere. It is a whole on its own account. Logic has for its content the determinations peculiar to the thinking activity itself which have no other ground than the Thinking. The *heteronomical* to it is what is simply *given to it* through Representation. Logic is, therefore, a great science. A distinction must, of course, be made between pure Thought and Reality, but Thought too has reality in so far as genuine actuality is understood by this term. In so far, however, as only sensuous external existence is meant by Reality, Thought has even a far higher reality. Thinking has therefore through its autonomy a content, namely itself. Through the study of Logic we also learn to think more correctly; for, since we *think the thinking of Thinking*, the mind thereby creates for itself its power. We become acquainted with the nature of Thinking and thus we can trace out the course in which it is liable to be led into error. It is as well to know how to give an account of one's deed. Thereby one gains stability and is not liable to be led astray by others.

2

Thinking is, in general, the apprehension and bringing together of the *manifold into unity*. The manifold as such belongs to externality in general, to Feeling and Sensuous Intuition.

Explanatory: Thinking consists in bringing the manifold into unity. When the mind thinks upon things it brings them into simple forms which are pure determinations of Spirit. The manifold is, at first, external to Thinking. In so far as we merely grasp the sensuous manifold we do not yet 'think', but it is the *relating* of the same that is properly called Thinking. The immediate seizing of the manifold we call **Feeling** or **Sensation**. When I Feel, I merely know something. In **Intuition**, however, I look upon something as external to me in space and time. Feeling becomes Intuition when it is determined in space and time.

3

Thinking is **Abstraction** in so far as intelligence, starting from concrete intuitions, neglects one of the manifold determinations, selects another, and gives to it the simple form of Thought.
Explanatory: If I neglect *all* the determinations of an object *nothing* remains. If, on the contrary, I neglect one and select another, the latter is then Abstract. The *I* [Ego], for example, is an abstract determination. I know of the Ego only in so far as I exclude all determinations from myself. This is, however, only a negative means. I negate the determinations of myself and leave myself as such. The act of Abstraction is the *negative* side of Thinking.

4

The **Content** of Representations are taken from Experience but the *form of unity* itself, and its further determinations, do not have their source in the Immediate as such but in Thinking.
Explanatory: The *I* [Ego] signifies, generally, *Thinking*. If I say: 'I think', this is something tautological. The Ego is perfectly simple. The Ego is a Thinking [activity] and that always. We cannot say, however, 'I am always thinking.' In principle yes, but what we Think is not always a Thought. But we could say, in the sense that we are Egos, 'We are always thinking', for the Ego is always the simple identity with itself and this simple identity with itself is Thinking. As Egos we are the ground of all our determinations. In so far as the externality [object] [*Gegenstand*] is thought it receives the form of Thought and becomes a *thought externality* [or *object*] [*einem gedachtes Gegenstand*]. It is made identical to the Ego, i.e. it is Thought.

5

This must not be understood as though this unity was first added to the manifold of external objects by Thinking and the linking was only introduced externally. On the contrary the unity belongs equally to the Object [*Objekt*] and, with its determinations, constitutes the proper nature thereof.

6

Thoughts are of three kinds:

(1) **The Categories**;
(2) **Determinations of Reflection**;
(3) **Concepts**.

The Doctrine of the first two constitutes **Objective Logic** or Metaphysics; the Doctrine of Concepts constitutes **Subjective Logic** or **Logic** proper.

Explanatory: Logic contains the system of pure Thinking; **Being** is (1) the Immediate, (2) the Inner; the thought determinations go back again into themselves. The objects of the common system of metaphysics are the Thing, the World, Mind, and God, which give rise to the different metaphysical sciences: Ontology, Cosmology, Pneumatology, and Theology.

(3) What the **Concept** presents us with is an *immediate being* [or *immediate existent*] [*ein Seiendes*] but at the same time is *essential*. Being stands in relation to Essence as the Immediate to the Mediate. Things simply are, but their Being consists in this: that they manifest their Essence. Being goes over into Essence; one can express it thus: Being presupposes Essence. But although Essence, in comparison with Being, appears as that which is *mediated*, yet, notwithstanding, Essence is the true *Origin*. In Essence, Being returns into its Ground; Being sublates itself in Essence. Being's essence has, in this way, *Become* or been *brought forth* [or *produced*] but what appears as having Become is rather the Origin. The Perishable has its basis in Essence and *becomes* out of Essence.

We form Concepts. These are something *posited* [*Gesetztes*] by us, but Concepts also contain the thing in its own proper nature. As compared with the Concept, Essence in its turn is the posited but the *posited* in this relation still stands for the true. The Concept is partly *subjective*, partly *objective*. The **Idea** is the union of subjective and objective. When we say, 'It is a mere Concept', we mean that it is without reality. Mere Objectivity on the other hand lacks the Concept. But the Idea states how reality is determined by the Concept. Everything actual is an Idea.

7

Science presupposes that the separation of itself from Truth is already overcome or that Spirit is no longer in a Phenomenal stage, as it was in the Science of Consciousness. Self-certainty embraces all that is an object of consciousness whether it be an external thing or a thought produced in the mind, in so far as Consciousness does not contain within itself all the moments of the **Being-in-and-for-itself**; (a) to be *in-itself*, or [have] simple equality with itself, (b) to have *Determinate Being* or determinateness, a *Being-for-other*, and (c) to be *for-itself*, i.e. in otherness to be simply returned into itself and with itself.

Science does not *seek* Truth but *is* in the Truth and *is* the Truth itself.

FIRST PART
BEING

FIRST SECTION
QUALITY

8

Quality is the immediate determinateness whose alteration is the transition into an opposite.

Being, Nothing, Becoming

9

Being is the simple empty immediacy which has its opposite in pure **Nothing** and their union is **Becoming**: as transition from Nothing into Being, it is *coming-to-be* [*Entstehen*]; the converse is *ceasing-to-be* [*Vergehen*].

('Sound common sense', as one-sided abstraction often calls itself, will not admit the union of Being and Nothing. 'Either Being *is*, or it *is not*. There is no third.' 'What is, does not Begin; what is not, also is not.' It asserts, therefore, the impossibility of a Beginning.)

Determinate Being

10

Determinate Being is a Being that has a specific [*bestimmtes*] Being, a Being which at the same time has a *reference* [*Beziehung*] *to an other* [and] hence to its Not-Being.

11

(a) Determinate Being is, consequently, divided within itself: firstly, it is *in-itself*; secondly, it is *relation to an other*. Determinate Being, thought with these two determinations, is **Reality**.

12

(b) Something has a reference to an other. The 'other' is a Determinate Being as the non-being of the something. Thus it has, in the first place, a **Boundary** or **Limit** and is *finite*. What something ought to be in-itself is called its **Determination**.

13

The way in which something is for an other or is connected with an other, and hence in-itself is also immediately posited by an other, is called its **Constitution**.

14

The way in which something is both an in-itself, as well as a being-for-other, is its *Determinateness* or **Quality**. The limit is not only the ceasing-to-be of the something but it belongs to the in-itself of the something.

15

(c) Through its Quality, through *what* it is, the something is subject to **Alteration**. It alters in so far as its determinateness comes into connection with another and thereby becomes a Constitution.

Being-for-itself

16

In as much as the Constitution is cancelled through Alteration, Alteration itself also is cancelled. Being, consequently, with this process, has retreated into itself and excludes otherness from itself. It is *for-itself*.

17

It is a **One**, which is related only to itself, and stands in a *repellent* relation towards others. [**Repulsion**]

18

This exclusion is at the same time a relation to others and hence is also an **Attraction**. No Repulsion without Attraction and vice versa.

19

Or, with the Act of Repulsion on the part of the One, *many* Ones are immediately posited. But the many Ones are not distinct from one another. Each One is what the other is. Hence their sublation, that is, their attraction, is equally posited.

20

The One is the Being-for-itself which is absolutely different from others. But since this difference, Repulsion, is sublated by Attraction, the difference is posited as sublated and therewith it has passed over into another determination: **Quantity**.

('Something' without its limit has no meaning. If I alter the limit of something it no longer remains what it is; if I alter the limits of a field it still remains a field as before though something larger or smaller. In this case I have altered its limit not as a field but as a 'quantum'. To alter its qualitative limit as a field means for example to make it a forest.)

SECOND SECTION
QUANTITY

21

Through Quality something is what it is. Through an alteration of Quality there is altered not merely a determination of something or of the Finite but the Finite itself. Quantity, on the contrary, is the determination which does not constitute the nature of the object itself; it is rather an *indifferent* distinction which may be altered while the object remains the same.

22

Quantity is the sublated Being-for-itself or the One. It is therefore an unbroken **Continuity** within itself. But since it equally contains the One it possesses also the moment of **Discreteness**.

23

(a) **Magnitude** is either Continuous or Discrete. But each of these two *kinds* of Magnitude contains Discreteness as well as Continuity in it and their difference is only this: that in Discrete Magnitude it is Discreteness which constitutes the main principle while in the Continuous it is Continuity.

24

(b) Magnitude or Quantity is, as limited quantity, a **Quantum**. Since this limit is nothing absolutely fixed it follows that a Quantum can be *increased* or *decreased*.

25
The limit of the Quantum, in the form of Being-within-itself, gives **Intensive Magnitude** and in the form of externality, gives **Extensive Magnitude**. But there is no Intensive Existence which does not also possess the form of Extensive Existence and conversely.

26
(c) Quantum has no intrinsically determined limit. There is, hence, no Quantum beyond which a larger or smaller could not be posited. The Quantum which is supposed to be the *last* one, the one beyond which there is supposed to be no greater or no smaller, is usually called the **Infinitely Great** or the **Infinitely Small**.

27
But in this shape it ceases to be a Quantum at all and is by itself equal to naught. It then has significance only as determination of a *Ratio* in which it no longer possesses any magnitude by itself but only a determination in relation to another. This is the more accurate concept of the **Mathematical Infinite**.

28
The **Infinite**, in general, when grasped in the form of an infinite progress, is the process of cancelling the limit, whether it be qualitative or quantitative, so that this limit counts as something positive and continually arises after its negation, but the limit, being grasped as a negation, is the **Genuine Infinite**, is the **Negation of the Negation**. In it the progress beyond the Finite does not posit again a fresh limit but, through the sublating of the limit, the existence is restored to equality with itself.

29
The sublating of Quantum in the Infinite means that the indifferent external determination which constitutes Quantum is sublated and becomes an 'inner' Qualitative determination.

THIRD SECTION
MEASURE

30
Measure is a specific Quantum in so far as it is not external but is determined by the nature of the object, by Quality.

31
In the alterations of a Quantum, in its increase or decrease which falls within its Measure, there enters likewise a specifying process in which the indifferent, external movement of magnitude up and down the scale is, at the same time, determined and modified by the nature of the thing itself.

32
When the Measure of a thing is altered the thing itself alters and ceases to be through the passing beyond its measure, [beyond] the particular something that it was; that is, increasing or decreasing beyond it.

SECOND PART
ESSENCE

33
Essence is Being which has returned into itself from its immediacy and whose determinations are sublated into a simple Unity.

FIRST SECTION
THE DETERMINATIONS OF ESSENCE

34
Essence shines [or is reflected into itself] and determines itself. But its determinations are in unity. They are only posited Being, that is, they are not immediately for-themselves but only such as remain in their unity. They are therefore **Relations**. They are Determinations of Reflection.

34a
Determinations, in so far as they belong to immediate Being and are not contained in an inner unity, become differentiated as inessentials from the Essence.

35
The essential determinations being contained in the unity of Essence, their Determinate Being is a *posited being* i.e. in their Determinate Being they are not immediate and independent but are mediated. They are therefore thought determinations in the form of Reflections.

36

(1) The first determination is the essential unity with itself: **Identity**. Expressed as a proposition, namely, as a universal determination, it is the proposition **A** = **A**, 'everything is identical with itself'; negatively [expressed, it is] the proposition of contradiction: '**A** cannot be at the same time **A** and **not-A**.'

37

(2) The [second] determination is **Difference**, of things which are indifferent to one another but distinguished through some determinate being or other. The proposition which it expresses is written: 'There are no two things which are perfectly alike.'

(3) As the determination of **Opposition**, as positive and negative, in which the determination of one is posited only by means of the determinateness of another, and each of these determinatenesses *is* only in so far as the other is but at the same time is only in so far as it is not the other. The proposition through which this is expressed reads: '**A** is either **A** or **not-A** and there is no third.' (The proposition *exclusii tertii*.)

38

(4) The third [determination], in which the posited determinations in general are sublated, is Essence, which is, in so far, **Ground**. The proposition of Ground reads, 'Everything has its *sufficient ground*.'

(Ground is that by which something is posited and thereby comes into existence; this is no transition into opposed determinations, like Becoming in Being, but in Ground there is unity of the connection. Although the posited Existence can at the same time be a shape different from its Ground, yet it must at the same time be contained in it.)

39

In so far as immediate Existence is regarded as something merely posited, it has returned into Essence or into its Ground. The former [i.e. Essence] is here the first, that from which we started, but in this return we retract that position and recognize the Ground rather as the first and essential.

40

The Ground contains that which is grounded by it according to its essential determinations. But the relation of the Ground to the grounded is a [unity] and not a transition into opposites, though the grounded existence has a different shape from its Ground, which is likewise an existence, and the chief determination is their common content.

SECOND SECTION
APPEARANCE

Thing

41
Ground is, in the first place, the simple unity of different determinations so that in the Ground they are not separated and apart from one another. In it they have the form of sublated [moments] and their subsistence is constituted by the Ground. This existing whole is a **Thing** of many **Properties**.

42
The Thing emerges from the Ground into Determinate Being, [into] Existence, in so far as this is the positing that has become self-identical and thus the restored immediacy, a being which is not itself immediate but can be called **Existence** [*Existenz*].

Existence is mediated by the sublated mediation; the Ground falls to the ground [*geht zu Grunde*] in its Existence; we think of the Ground as not being lost because, as regards its content, it remains.

43
The Properties of the Thing are determinations of its Existence which have an indifferent difference from one another and, equally, the Thing is, as simple identity with itself, undetermined and indifferent towards them as determinations.

The indifference of the enduring is the Thing, also expressed as: The Thing *is* presented [*vorher*], before [*ehe*] it exists.

44
Through Thinghood the determinations are identical with themselves and the Thing is nothing but this identity of its Properties with itself. Apart from its Properties, Thinghood has no truth [validity]. The Thing is thereby dissolved into its Properties as self-subsistent Matters.

45
Since, however, the Matters are united in the unity of a Thing, they interpenetrate each other reciprocally, are absolutely porous, and are

dissolved in each other. The Thing is consequently this contradiction within itself or it is posited as merely self-dissolving, as Appearance.

Appearance

46

(1) The self-identity of the Thing and of the matter is dissolved. Consequently the determinations have no being in-themselves but only in an other; they are only posited or they are **Appearance**.
(2) Self-identity in Appearance is indeterminate and merely capable of being determined, it is passive **Matter**. The identity of the determinations in their connection with one another constitutes the active side of Appearance, or **Form**.

47

Essence must appear, on the one hand, because Determinate Being is dissolved in its own self and retreats into its Ground: i.e. [into] negative Appearance; on the other hand, because Essence, as Ground, is a simple immediacy and therefore Being-in-General,

On account of the identity of Ground and the Existent there is nothing in the Appearance which is not in the Essence and, conversely, nothing in Essence which is not in the Appearance.

48

Since Matter is determined by Form both are presupposed as self-subsistent and independent of one another. But there is no Form at all without Matter and no Matter without Form. (Matter and Form generate each other *reciprocally*.)

49

Since the determinations manifest themselves also in the form of Independent Existence the relation of the same, as being determined through each other, constitutes the **Mutual Relation** [*Verhältniss*]. Eternity of Matter.

Relation

50

Form determines Matter. It is active towards Matter as towards an other. This activity is a reflecting of the determinations in two ways: (1) Form posits determinations in Matter and these determinations obtain a subsistence in Matter or they constitute the subsistence of Matter itself. But in this externality [belonging to Form] they remain connected with their unity or are reflected and Form simply remains in their unity with itself.

51

(2) Form in relating itself to Matter, at the same time, relates itself to it as to an other. But Matter is identical with itself. Form, therefore, in its relation to the self-identity, determines it or reflects itself in it, and this identity is only through this reflection. Matter is thus generated by the determining activity of Form. Matter, therefore, is presupposed by this activity but it is a presupposition which is sublated by the activity of Form and is made a result.

Form is finite in so far as it is opposed to Force and in it has its limit. Similarly Matter, outside of which is Form, is finite Matter. Form is related positively and negatively to Matter and to itself; (a) to Matter (a a) positively, posits its own determinations, (b b) negatively, sublates the indeterminateness of Matter; (b) to itself (a a) positively, posits its own determinations, reflection into itself; (b b) negatively, sublates its negative identity with itself; gives its determinations subsistence, materiality.

52

In this essential unity of Form and Matter, Form, as the necessary connection of their determinations, is the *law* [*Gesetz*] of Appearance.

Form and Matter are inessential in so far as they are separated from the Thing itself, from their unity.

What appears as posited under the determination of Form, as the Formed, constitutes the **Content** which is distinguished from the Form itself since this appears in relation to it as an external relation.

53

Since, moreover, the determinations posited by Form are identical with themselves, or are material, they appear as an independent existence and their connections with one another constitute Relation.

Here Form and Matter are distinguished not from one another but from their unity.

54

Relation is a connection of two sides which partly have an indifferent subsistence but partly each is only through the other and in this unity which determines both.

55

The determinations are posited firstly in the form of a Relation. Secondly, they are only *implicitly* these determinations of the Form and appear as an independent, Immediate Existence. They are in this respect a presupposed existence which internally in its own self already contains the totality of Form, which can have Existence only through that presupposed Determinate Being, or they are in so far *conditions*, and their relation is a Conditioned Relation.

56

In the conditions and in the conditioned relation, Appearance begins to return into Essence and Being-in-itself, but there still exists therein the difference of Appearance as such and of itself in so far as it is 'in-itself'.

57

(1) The immediate Conditioned Relation is the relation of **Whole** and **Parts**. The Parts, as existing on their own account outside of the Relation, are mere Matter and, in so far, not Parts. As Parts they have their determination only in the Whole and, in order to be Parts, they must also be capable on their own account of entering into this relation to the Whole; only then do the Parts constitute the Whole.

58

(2) The Whole, as the inner active Form, is **Force** [*Kraft*]. It has no external Matter as its condition but is in Matter itself. Its condition is only an external impetus which solicits it. The latter is itself the expression of a Force and requires to be solicited in order to be manifested. What we have then is a reciprocal conditioning and being conditioned which in the Whole is therefore unconditioned.

59

As regards content, Force in its expression exhibits what it is in-itself since as Form it contains within itself its determinations and there is nothing in its expression which is not in its Inner.

60

The content which is thus unconditioned is related to itself as **Inner** only [as] to itself as **Outer**; Inner and Outer are the same, only considered from different sides. The Inner is the totality of the determinations of the content as conditions which themselves have existence; their becoming Outer is itself their reflection into themselves, the taking of them together into the unity of a Whole which hereby acquires existence.

THIRD SECTION
ACTUALITY

Substance

61

Substance is the unconditioned content of Outer and Inner, absolutely self-subsistent Essence; unconditioned as regards the determinations of its content, since it is not conditioned by an other, and unconditioned in respect of Form since its externality is grounded in its own inwardness.

62

All determinations and conditioned existences are appearing determinations of substance and have an alterable and transient Determinate Being; they are **Accidents**. In their totality they constitute Substance.

63

Accidents exhibit, in their manifold variety, the determinations of the content of Substance in their essential nature in such a way that they run through the sphere of inessential circumstances, each of which is sublated in another, and what is preserved is only the simple substantial determination. Substance is the power which dominates the Accidents in so far as they sublate themselves in themselves but, at the same time, in thus sublating themselves they reveal what is Substantial.

64

Accidents, in so far as they are *implicitly* contained in the Substance, are possible. Substance itself is not possible but is Possibility itself.

65

Anything that is thought or simply imagined in the form of Being-in-itself or as not self-contradictory is called **Possible**; it is a Being-in-itself which is something only posited [and] not in-and-for-itself. A single determination has such a Possibility separated from Actuality.

Potentiating: Number sublates Accidentality (its immediate contingent being which can be equally 4 or 5, etc.), and, in this sublating, this altering, it manifests itself and becomes **Power** [*Macht*]. It is in the first place only contingent and immediate but the square and the cube are identical with themselves, their Being has become a Being-in-itself. They alter but they themselves determine their alteration [i.e. are] self-determination, Reflection-into-self, *actu* and *potentia*. Difference between Power and Possibility. I may not.

66

Something is *truly* Possible only as a totality of its implicit determinations. Whatever possesses this inner complete Possibility is not merely a posited being but absolutely and immediately **Actual**. The Possibility of substance is, therefore, its Actuality. (God, e.g., is not only generally but truly possible. His 'possibility' is a necessary one. He is absolutely Actual.)

67

The connection of Accidents in the Substance is their **Necessity**. (It is the unity of Possibility and Actuality.) Necessity is blind in so far as the connection is merely an inner one or in so far as the Actual is not already present as an implicit unity of its determinations, as End, but results only from their relation.

God is the **Absolute Idea of Reason**, not a posited or imagined Being, not something merely possible, He is the necessary Idea not posited by an alien thinking.

The knowledge of God is immediate and mediated; (a) [immediate,] as Reason's knowing of its Absolute, (b) mediated, as ascent from the finite which is merely contingent, possible, something merely posited, reflected in an other; His reflection into Himself is his 'actuality'. [We must not] speak of God's possibility as ground, as the true first, or as the positive. This possibility is the contingent world which is sublated in its own self, is reflected into itself out of the reflection in an other, actually *is* and manifests Actuality.

Cause

68

As Power, Substance is the manifestation of itself in the *coming-to-be* and *ceasing-to-be* of Accidents [arising and vanishing]. Active Substance, as original and primary, is turned against the Contingent as against an other and is **Cause** which acts on this other.

69

The activity of Substance consists in making its original content into an **Effect**, into a positivity which is in an alien existence. There is nothing in the Effect which is not in the Cause and Cause is cause only in the Effect.

A falling brick is the cause of a man's death, the miasma of a region is the cause of fevers; the first is primarily only cause of a pressure, the second only of excessive dampness. But the effect in something actual which has other determinations besides, leads to another result.

70

The Effect is (a) by means of an other of the Cause; this as activity disappears in the effect; (b) the other as Cause has disappeared but the Effect is posited, is *in* the other.

71

In respect of Form the Cause is distinguished from the Effect in such a way that Cause is the actuality which originally is spontaneously active, but the Effect is posited and in an other, as a determination in an other, in something Actual. It enters into a relation with the rest of the other's determinations and thereby receives a shape which no longer belongs to it as effect.

72

The Cause passes over into the Effect but, conversely, we go from the Effect to the Cause; this regress belongs in the first place to external reflection. Since the Cause itself has a specific content, is contingent and is to be posited as Effect, we obtain an infinite regress of a series of causes and effects. Conversely, in so far as that which suffers the effect is itself original it is a Cause and produces its effect in an other; the same series in an infinite progress.

(External reflection: the Cause is something other than the Effect, is difference of the something, absolute reflection, the same content, the same thing, [e.g.] rain and moisture, is only identity of the thing, in the effect is what is in the cause; we recognize one from the other, external identity, Form and Content or the thing exchange themselves; Cause and Effect are a difference of Form; Cause counts as the thing itself and then again only as Form. It is only in combination with that in which it is posited that the effect has actuality.)

Reciprocity

73

In so far as something receives into itself the effect but at the same time makes itself into a Cause and maintains itself in face of the effect as something external to it, it reacts and the reaction is equal to the effect [i.e. **Reciprocity**].

Causality has extinguished what is primary, the Cause, which, however, is transient. Therefore it does not necessarily give rise to another 'cause' and so on.

The Effect posited in another actuality becomes a Cause again; this is a negative action, i.e. the Effect is sublated.

74

The reaction takes place against the first Cause, which consequently is posited as Effect or is made into something posited through which nothing else happens except that it is now posited as what it is in-itself, namely, as not truly primary but transient.

75

Reciprocity then consists in this: that Effect becomes Cause and Cause becomes Effect. In this there is present a genuine primariness, in that, although the Cause does pass over into the Effect, into a positivity, yet, as regards the content, the thing itself, it remains the same and, also, as regards Form, it restores itself in its positivity.

76

In other words Reciprocity is the self-mediation in which what is primary determines itself or makes itself into a positivity; in this it is reflected into itself and only as this reflection-into-self is genuine primariness.

APPENDIX
[to Second Part]
THE ANTINOMIES

77

The categories are simple determinations but they do not constitute the first elements of the determination, unless, as antithetical moments, they are reduced to simplicity. Whenever such a category is predicated of a subject, and those antithetical moments are developed by analysis, the two are predicable of the subject and this gives rise to antinomial propositions, each of which has equal truth.

78

Kant especially has drawn attention to the Antinomies. However, he has not exhausted the antinomial character of Reason since he has expounded only a few of its forms. These are the following.

79

First Antinomy
(A) The Antinomy of the Finitude or Infinitude of the world in regard to Space and Time.

(1) The antinomy of the finitude or infinitude of the world in respect of Time.

Thesis: The world has a beginning in Time.

Proof: Let one assume that the world has no beginning in respect to Time; then, up to any given point of Time, an eternity has elapsed and consequently an infinite series of successive conditions of things in the world. The infinitude of a series consists, however, in this: that it can never be completed by successive synthesis. Therefore an infinite world series is impossible; hence a beginning of the world in Time is necessary.

Antithesis: The world has no beginning in Time and is infinite in respect to Time.

Proof: Let one suppose that the world had a beginning; then there would be assumed an empty Time before that beginning, a Time in which the world was not. In an empty Time, however, nothing can originate for in it there is no condition for existence, since one existence always has another existence as its condition or is limited by another existence. Therefore the world can have no beginning but every existence presupposes another and so on *ad infinitum*.

80

The proofs of this Antinomy, when reduced to a brief form, become the following direct antithesis:

(1) The world is finite in respect to Time; i.e. it has a limit. In the proof of the thesis such a limit is assumed, namely, the Now or some one given point of Time in which the infinite had come to an end, that is, was finite.
(2) Existence has a limit not in non-existence, in empty time, but only in an existence. The self-limiting somethings are also positively related to each other and the one has the same determination as the other. Since, therefore, each existence is limited by another or each is, at the same Time, a finite one, that is, such a one as must be transcended, it follows that the progress to infinity is posited.

81

The true solution of this Antinomy is this: Neither the limit nor the infinite is true by itself; for the limit is of such a kind that it must be transcended and the infinite is merely that in which the limit continually arises and which, beyond the limit, is only an empty negative. The true infinitude is the *Reflection-into-Self* and Reason contemplates not the temporal world but the world in its Essence and Concept.

82

(2) The Antinomy of the finitude or infinitude of the world in respect of Space

  Thesis: The world is limited in respect to Space.

Proof: Let one assume that it is unlimited; then it is an infinite given Whole of coexistent things and also, in general, an object. Such a Whole can be viewed as completed only through the synthesis of the parts therein contained. For this completion, however, infinite time is required which must be assumed as already elapsed which is impossible. Therefore an infinite aggregate of existing things cannot be viewed as a coexistent given Whole. The world is accordingly not infinite in Space but enclosed within limits.

  Antithesis: The world is unlimited in respect to Space.

Proof: Let one assume that the world is spatially limited; then it finds itself in an empty unlimited Space; it would, therefore, have a relation to this empty Space, i.e. a relation to no object, but such a relation, and therefore that of the world to empty Space, is nothing; therefore, the world is spatially infinite.

83

The proofs of these antinomial propositions really rest likewise on direct assertions.

(1) The proof of the thesis traces back the completion of the coexistent totality of the spatial world to the succession of Time in which the synthesis must happen and this is partly incorrect and partly superfluous, for in the spatial world the question is not of *succession* but of *coexistence*. Furthermore, when an already elapsed infinite Time is assumed a Now is assumed. Likewise in space a Here is to be assumed, that is, a limit of Space in general.

(2) Since the limit in Space in general is to be transcended it follows that the opposite of progress to infinity, the negative of the limit, is posited and, since this is essentially only a negative of the limit, it is conditioned by it. Hence the infinite progress is posited in the same way as in the previous Antinomy.

84

Second Antinomy
(B) The Antinomy concerning the simplicity or composite nature of substances

Thesis: Every composite substance consists of simple parts.

Proof: Let one assume that composite substances do not consist of simple parts. If, now, all composition or combination were thought away then there would be no composite part and, since there is also no simple part, nothing whatever, nor any substance, would remain. Consequently it is impossible to think away all composition. But the composite again does not consist of substances, for composition is only an accidental relation of them without which relation substances must subsist as enduring entities on their own account. Therefore the composite substance must consist of simple parts.

85

Antithesis: No composite thing in the world consists of simple parts, and there does not exist anywhere anything simple.

Proof: Let one assume that a composite thing consists of simple parts. Inasmuch as all external relation, consequently all composition of substance, is possible only in space, then the space which it occupies must consist of as many parts as the composite consists of. Now Space consists not of simple parts but of spaces, therefore every part of the composite must occupy a space. But the absolutely primary parts of everything composite are simple, therefore the simple occupies Space. Now since everything real which occupies Space contains a manifold whose parts are external to each other and is consequently composite, it follows that the simple would be a composite substance, which is self-contradictory.

86

The proof of the thesis contains the direct assertion that composition is an external relation or something contingent; hence the Simple is the Essential. The proof of the antithesis rests likewise upon the direct assertion that substances are essentially spatial and hence composite. In itself this Antinomy is the same as the previous one, namely, the positing of a limit and then the transcending of the same, a process which is involved in the concept of Existence.

87

Third Antinomy
(C) [The Antinomy concerning the antithesis of Causality according to natural laws and freedom]

Thesis: Causality according to natural laws is not the only causality from which the phenomena of the world can be derived. For an explanation of phenomena it is necessary also to assume a causality of freedom.

Proof: Let one assume that there is no other causality than according to the laws of nature; it follows that everything which happens presupposes a previous condition from which it proceeds, according to an invariable rule. Now that previous condition itself must have happened since, if it always had existed, its effect must always have existed. Therefore the causality through which something comes to pass is itself a something which has come to pass, and which again presupposes a previous condition and its causality and so on *ad infinitum*. There is therefore, at any given time, only a relative and no first beginning and hence, in general, no completeness of series on the part of the connected causes. The law of nature consists, however, precisely in this: that nothing happens without an efficient *a priori* cause. Therefore the proposition that all causality is possible only according to natural laws refutes itself and natural laws cannot be assumed as the only ones.

Antithesis: There is no freedom, but everything in the world comes to pass solely according to the laws of nature.

Proof: Let one assume that there is freedom, to wit, a power which can absolutely originate a state or condition and consequently a series of results thereof; then not only the series is originated through the spontaneity but the determination of this spontaneity itself is thus originated in such a manner that nothing can precede by which this action would be determined according to fixed laws. Each origination of an act, however, presupposes a state or condition of the cause which is not as yet active and a sheer first beginning of the act presupposes a state which has no causal connection whatever with the preceding state of the cause, i.e. which in no way results from it. Therefore absolute freedom is opposed to the law of causality.

88

This Antinomy, in general, rests upon the antithesis which the causal relation has in itself, namely, the cause (a) is an original cause, a first, self-moving cause but (b) is conditioned by something upon which it acts and then its activity passes over into the effect. Hence it is to be viewed as nothing truly original but as a posited. If (a) is held fast an absolute causality is assumed, a causality of freedom, but according to (b) the cause itself becomes something that has happened whereby it gives rise to the progress to infinity.

The true solution of this antinomy is *Reciprocity*; the cause which passes over into an effect has in this again a causal reaction whereby the first cause is reduced, in turn, to an effect or to something posited. In this reciprocity, consequently, is involved the fact that neither of the two moments of causality is absolute on its own account but that it is only the *closed circle* of the totality that is in-and-for-itself.

Thesis: An absolutely necessary Being belongs to the world.

Proof: The sensuous world, as the sum total of all phenomena, contains, at the same time, a series of alterations. Every alteration stands under its condition, under which it is necessary. Now every conditioned, in respect of its existence, presupposes a complete series of conditions up to the absolutely unconditioned, which alone is absolutely necessary. Therefore something absolutely necessary must exist if alteration exists as its result. This necessary something itself, however, belongs to the sensuous world; for assume that it exists outside of it, then the series of alterations in the world would derive their origin from it and yet this necessary cause itself would not belong to the sensuous world. Now this is impossible since the beginning of a series in time can be determined only through that which precedes it in time. The ultimate condition of the beginning of a series of alterations must exist in a time when this series did not as yet exist; hence this ultimate condition belongs to time and consequently to appearance or to the sensuous world itself. Therefore there is in the world itself something absolutely necessary.

Antithesis: There exists no absolutely necessary Being, either in the world or outside the world, as its cause.

Proof: Let one assume that the world itself, or something in it, is a necessary existence; then in the series of its alterations there would be a beginning which was unconditionally necessary and consequently without a cause, and this contradicts the dynamical law of the determination of all phenomena. Or else the series itself would be without a beginning and though in all its parts contingent and conditioned yet on the whole absolutely necessary and unconditioned; which is self-contradictory for the reason that the existence of an aggregate cannot be a necessary one if no single part of it possesses necessary existence. Furthermore, let one assume that there is an absolutely necessary cause of the world outside of the world, then it would initiate the existence of the changes in the world and their series. In beginning to act its causality would belong to time and hence to the sum total of all phenomena and hence not be outside of the world. Therefore there is neither in the world nor outside of it any absolutely necessary Being.

89

This antinomy contains, on the whole, the same antithesis as the previous one. With the conditioned a condition is posited and indeed an absolute condition, i.e. one which does not have its necessity in something else but is in its own self necessary. Since, however, it is connected with the conditioned it belongs itself to the sphere of the conditioned, to the world. According to the former side an absolutely necessary Being is posited but according to the latter only a relative necessity and hence contingency.

But since the condition belongs to the sphere of the conditioned, or rather is itself this whole sphere, it is itself only a conditioned. The conditioned has a condition, contains the condition in its concept absolutely separate. The condition [which] contains the conditioned in its concept is itself conditioned. The conditioned *has* a condition or *is* conditioned.

THIRD PART
THE CONCEPT

Subjective Logic

90

Subjective Logic no longer has for its object the category and the determination of reflection but Concepts. The category is Being in a determinateness, as limit which is mediated by the presupposition of an other. The Concept, on the other hand, is primary and original since its determination is its reflection into itself; in other words it is a simple whole which contains its determinations within itself and from which all its determinations flow.

91

Subjective Logic treats of three main objects,

(1) **The Concept**,
(2) **The End**,
(3) **The Idea**;

namely:

(1) the formal Concept or the Concept as such;
(2) the End, or the Concept in relation to its realization or its objectification;
(3) the Idea, the Real or Objective Concept.

FIRST SECTION
THE CONCEPT

92

Formal Logic contains:

(1) **The Concept**,
(2) **The Judgement**,
(3) **The Syllogism**.

[Concept]

93

(1) The **Concept** contains the moments of Individuality, Particularity, and Universality; it contains them as essential and distinct determinations. At the same time they are sublated in it and it is simple equality with itself.

94

Individuality is the negative reflection of the Concept into itself in which the determinations inhere as sublated, as moments, and which itself, as determined, excludes other determinations from itself or is absolutely determined.

95

Universality is the positive reflection of the Concept into itself in which the opposed moments do not exclude one another but which contains them in itself so that they are, at the same time, indifferent to it and remain undetermined in it.

96

Particularity is the relation to one another of Individuality and Universality; it is the Universal posited in a determination.

97

Just as these determinations, as moments of the Concept, are distinguished from one another, so too Concepts with a different content are distinguished as Concepts of the Universal, of the Particular and of the Individual.

98

The Universal subsumes or includes the Particular and the Individual under it, just as the Particular also subsumes the Individual under it. The Individual includes within it the Particular and the Universal and the Particular includes within it the Universal.

The Individual has the same or still other determinations than the Particular and the Universal. The same is true of the Particular in relation to the Universal. What therefore holds good of the Universal also holds good of the Particular and the Individual and what holds good of the Particular also holds good of the Individual, but not conversely.

99

But the Universal is more extensive than the Particular and the Individual and the Particular is more extensive than the Individual. The Universal transcends the Individual and the Particular. That is to say the Universal belongs not only to this Particular and this Individual but also to others and the Particular equally to several Individuals.

100

The Particular determinations which are subsumed under the same Universal are *coordinated* to each other. The same thing applies also to those which belong to the same Individual. But those determinations which are coordinated in a Universal cannot be coordinated in an Individual, it is exclusive.

101

The determinations coordinated in the Universal are *contradictory* in so far as one has the essential meaning of being what the other is not, or they are opposed as positive and negative. They are *contraries* in so far as they are posited as only different from one another, or one still has a positive determination which is not directly opposed to the other. However, the contradictory determinations necessarily also have the moment of indifference towards the others and the contrary determinations also have in them the moment of Opposition.

'Contradictory' does not mean merely opposed as such, like positive and negative, but that a content, an immediacy, is, *at the same time*, positive and negative.

An Opposite is the reference to an other, the entire content, the entire determination. 'Reference' [*Beziehung*] is here at one and the same time absolute Reflection into itself.

Judgement

102

(2) In the **Judgement** the absolute unity in which the moments are grasped together in the Concept is sublated. It [the Judgement] is the *relation* of the determinations of the Concept in so far as each at the same time is valid by itself as self-subsistent and independent of the others.

In the Judgement 'otherness' comes into the Concept. Judgement is a subjective affair; Subject and Predicate appear as indifferent, apart, external and are first brought together by us externally. *We* have here a Subject and here a Predicate which *we* attribute to the Subject. The Judgement must become *objective*. In Judgement there is a separation of Subject and Predicate, of the matter in hand and reflection. The Judgement destroys [*tötet*] the Concept.

103

The Judgement contains:

(1) The Subject as the side of Individuality or Particularity;
(2) The Predicate as the side of Universality, which is, at the same time, a determinate Universality, or also a Particularity in so far as it contains only one of the several determinations of the Subject;
(3) The simple contentless relation which the Predicate has to the Subject is the Copula.

104

The kinds of Judgement indicate the different stages in which the Predicate raises itself to essential Universality or the external relation of Subject and Predicate becomes an inner relation of the Concept. (The Subject is, firstly, in immediate identity with the Predicate, the two are one and the same determinateness of content; secondly, they are distinguished one from the other. The Subject is a more complex content than the abstract Predicate and is, in regard to form, contingent.)

105

In the Judgement the Predicate is immediately a property; namely, any one of the several determinatenesses of the Subject having only the immediate form of Universality: **Qualitative Judgement**.

106

(1) First we have the **Positive Judgement** when such a Predicate is attached to the Subject. This Predicate contains in respect of Content the moment of determinateness and in respect of Form the moment of Universality; and the Judgement, as regards Content, asserts: the Individual is determined thus; and, as regards Form: the Individual is Universal.

107

(2) The Judgement must also be negatively expressed in both respects:

(a) The Individual is also not so determined but differently;
(b) The Individual is not a Universal but a Particular. **Negative Judgement**.

108

In both respects this Judgement is still positive; in the first, only one determinateness is negated by the Subject, but it may have another of this Universal sphere; in the other respect the negation is only the restriction of Universality to Particularity.

109

The Negative, like the Identical Judgement, can be converted.

110

(c) However, the Individual is also not a Particular but the Individual is also only an Individual; consequently, not only any one determinateness of a Universal sphere but every such determinateness is sublated, and so generally the sphere itself: **Infinite Judgement**; in the positive form as identical, in the negative form as an absurd Judgement.

111

Judgements of Quantity contain a comparison of several Subjects in relation to a Predicate. The **Quantitative Judgement** is a *singular* whose Subject is *this* thing and should have as a Predicate a quality which belongs only to *this* Subject.

112

The **Particular Judgement** has *some* Predicates for the determination of the Subject, for which reason it is strictly indeterminate and what holds good for any such positive Judgement equally holds good of its negative.

113

The **Universal Judgement** has 'allness' for the determination of its Subject which is consequently a specific Particular Subject.

Necessity begins in the Universal Judgement. If *all* Subjects have *one* quality then we have Necessity.

Relation of Judgements or Judgements of Necessity

114

Judgements of Relation express an inner *necessary* reference of the Predicate to the Subject.

The **Categorical Judgement** has for Predicate the essence and general nature of the Subject.

115

The **Hypothetical Judgement** contains, along with complete diversity of the content of Subject and Predicate, their necessary reference to one another.

116

The **Disjunctive Judgement** has for its Subject something as a Universal sphere which is expressed in the Predicate in its complete particularization or in its various determinations, which together just as much belong to the Universal as they are mutually exclusive in respect of the Subject.

Modality of Judgements

117

The **Modality of Judgement** consists in the Predicate expressing the appropriateness or inappropriateness of a Subject to its Concept or general nature.

118

The **Assertoric Judgement** contains a mere assertion, in so far as the constitution of the Subject which is compared with its essence, or this essence itself, is not expressed. Hence the Judgement has a merely subjective validity.

119

Against the assertion of Assertoric Judgements therefore the opposite can equally be maintained; the Judgement therefore becomes *problematic* and expresses only the possibility that a Subject may or may not conform to the Concept. [**Problematic Judgement**]

120

As a Universal, therefore, the Subject is to be posited with a determination which contains the constitution in which lies the appropriateness or inappropriateness of the Subject to its general nature. In this way the Subject itself contains this relation of the Concept to existence expressed by the Predicate. – **Apodictic Judgement**.

Syllogism

121

(3) In the Judgement two determinations of the Concept are related immediately to each other. The **Syllogism** is the Judgement with its Ground. The two determinations are connected in the Syllogism by means of a third which is their unity. The Syllogism is, therefore, the complete *positedness* of the Concept.

122

According to the determined form, the two extremes of the Syllogism are the Individual and the Universal, and the Particular, since in it these two determinations are united, is their middle term. (If a determination **A** belongs to a determination **B**, but the determination **B** belongs to a determination **C**, then the determination **A** belongs to **C**.)

123

The relation of the two extremes (*termini extremi*) of the Syllogism to the Middle Term is an immediate relation and is a twofold one. It forms two Judgements (*propositiones praemissae*), each of which contains the moment of Particularity, the Middle Term (*terminus medius*). The one premiss contains, moreover, the extreme of Universality (*terminus major*) as Predicate (*propositio major*); the other contains the extreme of Individuality (*terminus minor*) as Subject (*propositio minor*); the relation of the two extremes, the Conclusion (*conclusio*), is Mediated.

124

The Mediation in the Syllogism presupposes an immediate relation and, obversely, the immediate relation is grounded therein and mediated; it is consequently present in the Concept as an indeterminateness, which in itself is Mediation.

SECOND SECTION
THE END OR THE TELEOLOGICAL CONCEPT

125

In the **End** that which is mediated or the result, is at the same time an immediate first or *ground*. What is produced, or posited through mediation, has the act of producing and its immediate determination for presupposition, and, conversely, the act of producing happens on account of the result which is the ground, and hence is itself the first determination of the activity.

126

The **Teleological Act** is a syllogism in which the same whole in subjective form is brought into unity with its objective form, the Concept with its reality, through the mediation of Teleological Activity, or the concept is ground of a reality determined by it.

127

External Purposiveness exists in so far as something possesses its concept, not in itself, but is linked to it by another, by an end, as its outer form.

128

There is Internal Purposiveness when an existence has its concept within itself and at the same time is end, means and self-realizing and realized End in its own self.

THIRD SECTION
THE IDEA OR THE ADEQUATE CONCEPT

129

The **Idea** is the unity of the **Concept** and **Reality**, the Concept in so far as it determines its own Reality or Actuality which is what it ought to be and which itself contains its Concept.

130

(a) The Idea, in so far as the Concept is immediately united with its Reality and does not, at the same time, distinguish itself from it and raise itself out of it, is **Life**. The same exhibited as liberated from all the conditions and limitations of contingent existence is the **Beautiful**.

131

(b) In the Idea of Cognition and Practical Activity the Concept stands opposed to Reality, or the subjective to the objective, and their union is brought about. In Cognition, Reality lies at the basis as the *first* and as Essence, to which the Concept is to make itself conform in order to be Truth; Practical Activity, on the other hand, has the Concept, as Essence, lying at its base and makes actuality conform to it so that the good may be brought about.

132

(c) The absolute Idea is the content of **Science**, namely, the consideration of the universe as in absolute conformity with the Concept, or the Concept of Reason, as it is in-and-for-itself and as it is in the objective or real world.

THE SCIENCE OF THE CONCEPT
[For the Higher Class]

1
Objective Logic is the Science of the Concept *in itself*, or the Science of the Categories. **Subjective Logic**, of which we treat here, is the Science of the Concept as Concept or of the Concept of something. It is divided into three parts:

(1) **The Science of the Concept**
(2) **The Science of its Realization**
(3) **The Science of the Idea.**

FIRST PART
SCIENCE OF THE CONCEPT

CONCEPT

2
The **Concept** is the Universal which is at the same time determinate; that which remains in its determination is the same Whole or Universal or it is the determinateness which grasps together within itself the different determinations of an object as a unity.

3
The moments of the Concept are Universality, Particularity and Individuality. The Concept is their unity.

4
The **Universal** is this unity as a positive, self-equal indeterminate unity; the **Particular** is the determination of the Universal but such that it is sublated in the Universal, i.e. the Universal remains in it what it is; **Individuality** is the negative unity or the determination which gathers itself up into a unity by determining itself.

5

The Universal includes *under it* the Particular and Individual; so likewise the Particular includes under it the Individual; on the other hand the Individual includes *in it* the Particular and the Universal and the Particular includes *in it* the Universal. The Universal is more *extensive* than the Particular or Individual but the latter are more *comprehensive* than the Universal, which for the reason that it is included in the Individual, is again a determinateness. The Universal *inheres* in the Particular and Individual while the latter are *subsumed* under the Universal.

6

Since the Concept contains in itself the moments of Individuality, Particularity and Universality, it is variously determined with regard to its content and is the comprehension of something Individual, Particular or Universal.

7

The particularization of the Universal, i.e. determinations which have one and the same common sphere, these, and likewise the Individuals which are subsumed under the same Particular or Universal, are said to be *coordinate*. What is subsumed is also said to be *subordinate* to that under which it is subsumed.

8

The coordinated Particular determinations of the Universal are opposed to one another and, when one is taken as the negative of the other, they are *contradictory*, but when the other also has positivity, and through this falls within the same general sphere as the former, they are opposed merely as *contraries*. Such determinations, coordinated in the Universal, cannot coexist in the Individual, but those which are coordinated in the Individual are (merely) *different*, i.e. they do not have in their difference the same general sphere, and in their harmony with the Individual are in accord.

9

The coordinate determinations of the Universal considered in more detail are (a) the one is the negative of the other in general, without regard to the question whether they have the same general sphere or not, and, in so far as they have the same sphere in common and the one determination is positive the other negative, so that this negativity toward each other constitutes their nature, they are (b) properly termed *Contradictories*; in so far as they stand in opposition in the same common sphere or the one is also positive in the same sense as the other, and each consequently can be called positive as well as negative in relation to the other, they are (c) *Contraries*.

10

With the determination of Contrariety, which is indifferent as regards the antithesis of positive and negative, they are *no longer determined by an other* but are *determined in-and-for-themselves* whereby the mutual participation of the same sphere has vanished and individuality imposed, whose determinations differ from each other without a common sphere and are thereby determined in-and-for-themselves.

JUDGEMENT

11

The **Judgement** is the presentation of an object as unfolded into the three moments of the Concept. It contains it (a) in the determination of Individuality as **Subject**; (b) in its determination of Universality or its **Predicate**, whereby the subject can also stand in relation to the Predicate itself as Individuality to Particularity and as Particularity to Universality; (c) in the simple contentless relation of the Predicate to the Subject, the *is*, the **Copula**.

12

The Judgement is to be distinguished from the **Proposition**: in the latter something quite individual, an occurrence, is affirmed of a Subject or also, as in general propositions, something is affirmed of the Subject as having a necessary connection with it and which it becomes or to which it essentially stands in opposition. Since in the Concept the moments are grasped as in a unity so too in the Judgement as in the presentation of the Concept, although there is determination, there is no becoming or antithesis. The inferior determination, the Subject, rises to the Universality which differs from it, i.e. to the Predicate, or *is* it immediately.

13

In Logic the Judgement is considered according to its pure form without regard to any specific empirical content. Judgements are classified by the relation in which the Subject and Predicate stand to each other, in how far their relation is through and in the Concept or is a relation of objectivity to the Concept. Upon the character of this relation depends the higher or absolute Truth of the Judgement. **Truth** is the agreement of the Concept with its objectivity. In the Judgement there begins this presentation of the Concept and its objectivity and with it the sphere of Truth.

14

In as much as the Judgement is the presentation of an object in the different moments of the Concept so, conversely, it is the presentation of the Concept in its existence; not so much on account of the specific content which the moments of the Concept have as because, in the Judgement, these latter issue forth from their unity. Just as the whole Judgement presents the Concept in its existence so this difference becomes again the form of the Judgement itself. The Subject is the object and the Predicate is the Universality of the same which is to express it as Concept. The movement of the Judgement through its different kinds raises this Universality to a higher stage, wherein it comes to correspond as nearly to the Concept as is possible for it in so far as it is simply a Predicate.

A   *Quality of Judgements, or the Judgement of Inherence*

15

The Predicate in the most elementary [*unmittelbar*] form of the Judgement is a property which belongs to the Subject in such a manner that although it stands in relation to it as Universal in general yet, at the same time, it is only a Particular existence of it which, as such, has several determinatenesses. Universality, the Predicate, has here the meaning only of an immediate (or sensuous) Universality, a mere possession in common with others.

16

In the **Qualitative Judgement** the Predicate is just as well something Universal, which side constitutes the form of the Judgement, as a specific quality of the subject, which appears as content. According to the former side the Judgement takes as its pure **Form**: 'the Individual is a Universal'; according to the latter, and the **Content**: 'the Individual is determined thus', and this is the **Positive Judgement** in general. ('This is good'; 'This is bad'; 'This rose is red'; 'This rose is white', etc.)

17

For the reason that (a) the Individual is equally not Universal and (b) the Subject has other determinations besides *this one*, the Qualitative

Judgement must also be expressed negatively in both respects; hence arises the **Negative Judgement**. ('This is not good'; 'This is not bad'; 'This rose is not red but white [or] yellow, etc.', 'This rose is not white but red', etc.)

18

According to **Form**, therefore, this Judgement is: *The Individual is not a Universal but a Particular*; according to **Content**: *The Individual is not thus but otherwise determined*. In both respects this Negative Judgement is at the same time also Positive. In the first respect the negation is only the limitation of the Universality to Particularity; in the other respect only some one determinateness is negated and through this negation the Universality, or its higher sphere, makes its appearance.

19

Finally, according to Form, the Individual is not a mere Particular, for Particularity is more extensive than Individuality, but the Individual is only the Individual and this is the **Identical Judgement**.

Conversely, according to Content the Subject is not only not this Particular determinateness, but also not merely any other determinateness. Such a content is too narrow for the Subject. Through this negation of the determinateness the entire sphere of the Predicate and the positive relation which subsisted in the preceding Negative Judgement is sublated and this gives the **Infinite Judgement**.

20

That Identical as well as the Infinite Judgements are no longer Judgements. More precisely this means that the relation which exists between the Subject and Predicate in the Qualitative Judgement is sublated, which relation was this: that there was expressed only some one of the immediate determinatenesses of its Being, a determinateness to which belonged only a superficial generality. In the Infinite Judgement a Universality is demanded which is not only a single determinateness. The afore-mentioned Identical Judgement states that the Subject is determined in-and-for-itself and in its determination has returned into itself.

21

In the Identical and Infinite Judgements the mutual relation of Subject and Predicate is sublated. This is to be taken first as that side of the Judgement according to which Subject and Predicate, being abstracted from their difference by the Copula, can be regarded as standing in a relation of identity. In this respect the Positive Judgement can become inverted in so far as the Predicate is taken only in the same extent of meaning as the Subject is.

22

The Negative Judgement contains the separation of a determinateness from its Subject in such a manner that the Subject is still related positively to the Universal, though not expressly stated, sphere of the determinateness. Where the negated Predicate is made the subject that Universal sphere falls away and leaves only the non-identity of two determinations in general and it is indifferent which of them is made Subject or which Predicate. The Negative Judgement, and also the Identical Judgement, can therefore be *inverted* without altering it.

B Quantity of Judgements, or Judgements of Reflection

23

Where judgements can be inverted the distinction of Subject and Predicate is ignored. This distinction, however, since it is now sublated as qualitative, is to be taken Quantitatively.

24

Since the single determinatenesses which the Predicate contained cancel themselves the Predicate has to include the manifold determinations of the Subject taken together. Through this circumstance the *universality* ceases to be a mere *community* [*eine blosse Gemeinschaftlichkeit*] with others. It is the Subject's *own* universality, which thus implies that the Subject has returned into itself in its predicate.

25

Such a judgement is consequently a **Judgement of Reflection**, since Reflection generally implies advancing to several determinations of an object and grasping them together in a unity.

26

In so far as the identity of the Subject with the Predicate makes its appearance the Subject is a Universal which is Subject through first confining it to Individuality. The Qualitative Judgement is therefore a *singular* which has in the determination of the Subject *complete* Individuality and is *this* Universal.

27

A **This** is determined in infinitely manifold ways, i.e. it is indefinitely determinable. The Predicate of Reflection, since it is a complex, expresses not only the general determination of *one* This but also of *other* This's, that is to say, the Singular Judgement passes over into the Particular [Judgement].

28

The Particular Judgement, in which the Subject is determined as *some*, is only a Determinate Judgement which can be expressed immediately just as well positively as negatively.

29

The Subject receives its complete determination, according to extent of form, through *All-ness* in the Universal Judgement. Since All-ness enters in place of Particularity, and has at the same time the extent of the latter, the extent of the content of the Subject must be limited accordingly.

30

The Subject becomes through this partly a Particular as regards its Predicate; partly there enters a relation of necessity between Subject and Predicate.

C *Relation of Judgements, or Judgements of Necessity*

31

Through the cancelling of the qualitative and quantitative determinations the *unity of the content* of Subject and Predicate is posited, which latter therefore *differ only through their form*, so that the same object is posited at one time merely as Subject, at another as Predicate.

32

Since the Subject is a Particular something as opposed to its Predicate, conversely the *Subject is now*, in contradistinction to the Qualitative Judgement, a *determinateness of the Predicate* and immediately subsumed under [it]. The Universality of the Predicate expresses, therefore, not merely a complex of determinatenesses of the Subject, like the Predicate of Reflection, but the Universal inner nature of the subject, and this is the **Categorical Judgement**. ('The body is heavy.' 'Gold is a metal.' 'Mind is rational.')

33

In so far as Subject and Predicate are also distinguished their unity must also be expressed as *unity of contraries*, i.e. as a *necessary* relation, and this is the **Hypothetical Judgement**.

34

The Identity of content, which is found in the Categorical Judgement and the Relation of contraries to others in the Hypothetical Judgement, is united in the **Disjunctive Judgement**, in which the Subject is a Universal sphere or is considered in regard to such a one and this [Universal sphere] constitutes the Predicate, and the *Particularization* or various determinations of the Predicate express this. Of these the one as well as the other belongs to the Universal. According to their Particularization and in respect to the subject, however, they *exclude each other*.

D   *Modality of Judgements, or Judgements of the Relation of the Concept to Existence*

35

In the Disjunctive Judgement an existence is posited in the complete moments of the Concept. **Modality of Judgements** consists in this: that an existent thing is related to its Concept as such and the Predicate expresses the *appropriatenes* or *inappropriateness* of the two.

36

The first Judgement of Modality is the **Assertorical [Judgement]** which contains a mere *assurance* in as much as only the *constitution* or *nature* of the Subject which is to be compared with the Concept is expressed and not the Concept itself; hence this judgement has at first only a subjective confirmation. ('This deed is bad', 'This remark is true.')

37

Against the assurance of the Assertorical Judgement, therefore, the *opposite proposition* may just as well be asserted; the Predicate expresses *only one* of those opposite determinatenesses of which the subject, considered as a Universal sphere, contains both. This judgement, therefore, passes over into the **Problematical [Judgement]**, which expresses merely the *possibility* of the conformity or non-conformity of the given existence to the Concept.

38

The Universality of the Subject is, therefore, posited with a limitation which expresses the constitution or nature in which lies the conformity or non-conformity of the given existence with the Concept. The Predicate expresses nothing else than this identity or non-identity of the constitution or nature and the Concept of the object. This is the **Apodictic Judgement**.

SYLLOGISM

39

The **Syllogism** is the complete exhibition of the Concept. It contains, as such, **The Judgement with its Ground**. There are in it two determinations which are united by means of a third which is their unity. It is a Concept present as a unity (the middle term of the Syllogism) and in its diremption (the extremes of the Syllogism).

40

The relation of the two extremes of the Syllogism to the middle term is an immediate one; their relation to each other, however, is mediated through the middle term. The former, the two immediate relations, are the judgements which are called **Premisses**. The relation which is mediated is called the **Conclusion**.

41

In the first place the Syllogism expresses its moments through the mere *form* in such a manner that the middle term is a peculiar determinateness as opposed to the extremes and the ground or unity of the moments is still a merely *subjective* one. That which is really primary is in this case deduced and has the signification of a result.

A *Syllogisms of Quality or of Inherence*

42

The form of this Syllogism I–P–U (Individual–Particular–Universal), that the *Individual* is connected with the *Universal* through the *Particular*, is the general rule of the Syllogism as such. In the first, immediate, Syllogism, the Particular or the middle term is a *quality* or determinateness of the Individual and likewise the Universal is a determinateness of the Particular. Therefore a transition can be made from the Individual through *another* one of its determinations, of which it has several, to another Universal and so likewise from the Particular to another Universal, since the Particular also contains within itself different determinations. Accordingly this Syllogism does appear to be correct so far as its *form* is concerned but according to its *content* is arbitrary and contingent. ('Green is a pleasant colour; this leaf is green; hence it is pleasant.' 'The sensuous is neither good nor bad; but man is a sensuous being; hence he is neither good nor bad.' 'Bravery is a virtue; Alexander possessed bravery; hence he was virtuous.' 'Drunkenness is a vice; Alexander was addicted to drunkenness; hence he was vicious.' etc.)

43

According to form the two premisses are immediate connections. The form of the Syllogism contains, however, the demand that they should *also be mediated* or, according to the common expression, the premisses should be *proved*. But the proof through this form of the Syllogism would be only a *repetition* of that form and thus the same demand would recur again *ad infinitum*.

44

The mediation, that is of Particularity and Universality, must therefore be brought about through the moment of Individuality. This gives the second form of the Syllogism: **U–I–P**. This Syllogism is correct in the first place only in so far as the judgement **U–I** has validity. In order that this may be the case **U** must be Particular. In this way the Individual is not really the middle term. The Syllogism is brought back to the form of the first but the conclusion is Particular. This Syllogism has however, in general, the signification, in contradistinction to the other, that immediate determinations or qualities are connected through Individuality and in so far contingently.

45

The Individual connected with the Particular through the *Universal* gives the third form of the Syllogism: **P–U–I**. The Universal is here the mediating determination and in both premisses the Predicate. But it does not follow that two determinations are the same because they inhere in the same Individual; it follows rather that the two determinations are subsumed under the same Universal and not that they can be linked as Subject and Predicate. Only in so far as the major premiss is *negative*, and therefore can be inverted, does this Syllogism admit of reduction to the first and consequently possess the correct form. ('No finite being is holy; God is no finite being; therefore God is holy.')

46

The objective signification of this Syllogism is that the union of Particularity with Individuality has its ground only in the identical nature of the two.

47

In the series of these Syllogisms each of the three determinations has in succession constituted the middle term. The reduction of the second and third syllogistic forms is the *sublating* of the *Qualitative*.

Although each immediate relation of the first Syllogism is mediated by the succeeding ones, yet each of the latter presupposes the preceding one, i.e. the mediated unity presupposes the immediate identity.

B   *Syllogisms of Quantity or Reflection*

48

The immediate non-qualitative Syllogism is the **Mathematical Syllogism**. The middle term of this Syllogism is only a term that is *equal* to the two others. As a proposition it is expressed thus: If two magnitudes are equal to a third, they are equal to each other.

49

Secondly, in the **Quantitative Syllogism**, Individuality, not as *one* Individual but as *all Individuals*, constitutes the middle term. In so far as some one quality belongs to all this quality is expressed as quality of that Universal sphere or of the *genus* itself to which the Individuals belong. This is the **Syllogism of Induction**.

50

The Syllogism in which the *Universal* is the middle term infers through *analogy* that, in the case of two subjects which are the same according to their general determinations, a Particular determination which belongs to one *also* belongs to the other.

(a) Several Individuals have a common nature;
(b) *One of the Individuals has a certain quality*;
(c) Therefore the other Individuals too have this quality.)

(In the case of Induction the question arises what ought to be the Subject or Predicate in the conclusion; e.g. 'What moves itself with freedom is an animal', or 'An animal is what moves itself with freedom.' 'The lion is a mammal', or 'What a mammal is, is a lion.' In the case of Analogy, on the contrary, the mediation lies in the fact that another Individual has the same common nature. While in the case of Induction the Particular determinateness of the common nature is grounded in the Individual, Analogy infers from the common nature the Particular determinateness of the Individual; e.g. 'The earth has motion, the moon is an earth; therefore the moon has motion.' 'Jupiter and the Earth are planets; the Earth has inhabitants; therefore Jupiter has inhabitants.')

C *Syllogisms of Relation*

51

The **Categorical Syllogism** has for middle term the Universality or the nature of the Individual subject, of which as such an essential property is expressed and is linked with this subject.

52

The **Hypothetical Syllogism** expresses as the ground of an existence another existence. If **A** is, then **B** is: but **A** is; therefore **B** is. The determinations are no longer in relation as Individual, Particular and Universal, but a determination, **B**, which in the first place is only implicit, or possible, is connected with existence through **A** as middle term which is existent as well as ground.

53

In the **Disjunctive Syllogism** the ground that a determination is connected with a Subject consists in this: that one part of the Particular determinations of a Universal sphere do not belong to it and consequently the rest do belong to it or, when the determination is separated from the subject, conversely **A** is either **B**, **C**, or **D** but it is not **B** or **C**; therefore it is **D**.

54

The middle term is therefore the Subject as a Universal sphere in its complete Particularization and contains, at the same time, the excluding or positing of a part of these its determinations. The Subject as a Universal is in itself the possibility of several determinations. From its Universality or possibility a transition is made to its determinateness or actuality.

55

From a survey of the forms of the Syllogism we see that:
(1) In the *Qualitative* Syllogisms the moments have validity in their

qualitative difference. They need therefore a mediating link which is their immediate unity but this falls outside of them.
(2) In the *Quantitative* Syllogisms the qualitative difference of the moments is suppressed and with it the mutual relation and the difference of mediated and immediate are obliterated.
(3) In the Syllogisms of *Relation* the mediation contains at the same time immediacy. From this therefore has emerged the Concept of an Immediacy of nature or of qualitative difference which, at the same time, is absolute mediation, end and process.

SECOND PART
REALIZATION OF THE CONCEPT

56
In Judgement, as in the Syllogism, the Concept is in immediate reality, in the indifferent existence of the Subject and predicate, or the extremes of the Syllogism are opposed to each other and to the middle term. The **Objective** consists in this: that these moments become in themselves the Whole, so that their Immediacy is precisely this, to be the Whole.

57
In the **End** that which is outcome and result is at the same time the immediately active ground. It is, as something subjective, separated from the external existence which is present and the activity consists in the translation of the subjective form into objectivity. In this transition the End returns into its Concept.

58
The Syllogism of the purposive act has three moments: (1) the subjective End, (2) mediation and (3) the realized End. Each of these moments is the *totality* of the determinations of the Syllogism.

59
(1) The *subjective* End contains: (a) the indeterminate *free activity* of a Subject in general, which (b) determines itself or Particularizes its Universality and gives itself a specific content, and (c) it has the moment of Individuality, in accordance with which it is negative toward itself, *sublates* the *subjective* and produces an *external* existence independent of the subject.

60

(2) **Mediation** or the transition into objectivity has two sides in it: (a) that of *Objectivity*; this is an external thing as *means*, which, put under the power of the subject, becomes a means and by it is turned against external existence, (b) the side of *Subjectivity* is the mediating activity which, on the one hand, brings the means into relation to the End and subordinates it thereto and, on the other hand, turns it against the Other and by cancelling the determinations of the externality gives the End a real existence.

61

(3) The *realized* End is: (a) existence of the objectivity in general, (b) not, however, only an immediate Existence but a posited and mediated one and (c) of the same content as the End.

62

The defect of this teleological relation is the immediate existence of each of the three moments which enter into relation, for which, therefore, the relation and the determinations which those moments receive in it are externally brought together. The entire movement of this realization of the Concept is therefore altogether a *subjective* Act. As *objective* Act, the realization is the *Process* as inner relation of the moments of the Syllogism according to their peculiar nature. In **Process** actual objects stand in relation as independent extremes, whose inner determination however is that it *is* through the mediation of others and is linked with them.

63

(1) In the **Sphere of Mechanism** objects are united or altered by a third force so that this union or alteration does not lie in their nature beforehand but is external or contingent to them and, consequently, they remain in it independent of each other.

64

(2) In the **Chemical** sphere each of the two exremes is: (a) a determinate existence [*Dasein*] which, at the same time, is essentially opposed to the other, (b) as in opposition *in itself* a relation to the other. It is not only itself but it is determined as something which exists only in union with the other, or its nature is tensed within itself and activated against the other. (c) The unity of the extremes is the *neutral* Product which constitutes the ground of their relation and of their entry into the process but this unity is present in them only as an implicit

relation. It does not exist freely for itself anterior to the process. This is the case in Teleology.

65

(3) The higher unity is therefore that the activity maintains itself in the Product, or that *the Product is self-producing*, hence the neutralizing of the moments is equally their diremption, or the extinguishing of the process in the union of the extremes is at the same time the rekindling of it. The activity of this productive Product is consequently **Self-Maintenance**. It produces only itself and yet it already exists.

THIRD SECTION
SCIENCE OF THE IDEA

66

The **Idea** is the objectively True or the adequate Concept in which existence is determined by its Immanent Concept and in which Existence, as self-producing product, is in an external unity with its End. The Idea is not an actuality which corresponds to some external notion or other but one which corresponds to its own Concept; which, therefore, is in such a form as it ought to be in-and-for-itself and contains this its Concept. The **Ideal** is the Idea considered from the side of Existence but as an existence which conforms to the Concept. It is, therefore, the Actual in its highest truth. In contradistinction to the expression Ideal one would call Idea rather the True considered from the side of the Concept.

67

There are three Ideas:

(1) **The Idea of Life**;
(2) **The Idea of Cognition and of the Good**, and
(3) **The Idea of Science** or of **Truth** itself.

THE IDEA OF LIFE

68

Life is the Idea in its immediate existence whereby it enters the field of Appearance or of Being which is changeable and variously and externally determined and confronts an inorganic Nature.

69

As the immediate unity of the Concept and Existence, Life is a Whole of which the Parts are nothing by themselves but exist only through and in the Whole and equally the Whole *is* through the Parts. It is an *organic System*.

IDEA OF COGNITION AND OF THE GOOD

70

In this Idea the Concept and Actuality fall asunder. The former, on the one hand, empty by itself, is to receive its determination and filling from Actuality; on the other hand, Actuality should receive its determination from the independent determination of the Concept.

A   Cognition

71

Cognition is the relation of the Concept and Actuality. The Thinking, which in-itself is filled only with itself and is in so far empty, becomes, through Cognition, replete with a particular content and this is raised from [mere] Existence to a more universal Representation.

72

Definition expresses, of an object which stands in relation to it as an individual or a particular, its *genus* as its universal Essence and the particular determinateness thereof through which it is *this* object.

73

Classification expresses of a *genus* or universal in general, a race, or an order, etc., the particulars in which it exists as a manifoldness of species. These particularizations which are contained in a unity must flow from a common ground of division.

74

Cognition is partly Analytical, partly Synthetical.

75

Analytical Cognition proceeds from a Concept, or a concrete determination, and develops only the manifoldness of the immediate or identical simple determinations which are therein contained.

76
Synthetical Cognition, on the contrary, develops the determinations of a Whole which are not immediately contained in it and do not flow from it in an identity but have the form of 'difference' towards each other and it [synthesis] shows the necessity of their specific relation to each other.

77
This happens through **Construction** and **Proof**. Construction exhibits the Concept or proposition, partly in its real determinations, partly on behalf of the proof; it exhibits this its reality in its division and dissolution through which its transition into the Concept begins.

78
Proof takes up the dissolved Parts and produces, through comparison of their relations to one another, that union of them which in the Theorem constitutes the expressed relation of the Whole. Or it shows how the real determinations are moments of the Concept and exhibits in their reciprocal relation the Concept in its totality.

79
In this Cognition, which in its strictest form is the geometrical, (a) the construction does not proceed from the Concept but is a contrivance that has been discovered which shows itself to be adopted with special reference to the proof; in other cases it is only an empirical description. (b) In the Proof, instead of analytical determinations otherwise well known or settled, synthetical propositions are brought in from outside and the subject matter under consideration subsumed or united under them. The Proof thereby receives the appearance of contingency since it presents for insight only *a* necessity [and] not the object's own process and inner necessity.

B   The Ought or the Good

80
In the Idea of Cognition the Concept is sought and it ought to be adequate to the object. Conversely in the Idea of the Good the Concept counts as primary and as the implicit End which *ought* to be realized in Actuality.

81

The **Implicit Good**, since it has yet to be realized, stands in opposition to a world and a Nature which does not correspond to it and which has its own laws of necessity and is, therefore, *indifferent* to the laws of freedom.

82

The **Intrinsically Good** is an absolute End in-itself to be carried out without any regard to consequences since it has committed to its charge an actuality which is independent of it and may utterly thwart it.

83

At the same time, however, it is implied that in-itself Actuality *harmonizes* with the Good, or that there is faith in a moral order of the world.

THE IDEA OF KNOWING OR TRUTH

84

Absolute Knowing is the Concept which has itself for object and content and consequently is its own reality.

85

The Process or the *Method* of the Absolute Knowing is both analytical and synthetical. The development of what is contained in the Concept, Analysis, is the evolution of different determinations which are contained in the Concept but are not as such immediately given, and for this reason the procedure is at the same time synthetical. The exposition of the Concept in its real determinations here proceeds from the Concept itself, and what constitutes the proof in ordinary cognition is here the return into unity of the moments of the Concept out of the diversity into which they have gone; this result is therefore **Totality**: the Concept which has become fulfilled and is its own content.

86

This mediation of the Concept with itself is not only a *Process of Subjective Cognition* but equally *the own inner movement of the subject matter itself*. In Absolute Cognition the Concept is equally the *beginning* and is also the *result*.

87

The progress to further Concepts, or to a new sphere, is likewise guided and necessary by what has preceded. The Concept which became reality is at the same time again a unity which must exhibit the movement of the realization in itself. But the development of the antithesis contained in it is not a mere dissolution into the moments from which it has originated, these moments now have another form through the fact that they have gone through the unity. In the new development they are now posited as that which they are through their relation to one another. They have received, consequently, a new determination.

4
THE PHILOSOPHICAL ENCYCLOPAEDIA
[For the Higher Class]

1

An **Encyclopaedia** has to consider the whole range of the sciences according to the subject matter and fundamental concepts of each.

2

The multiplicity of experiences of a universal object summarized in the unity of general conceptions and the thoughts generated in considering its essence, constitute in their connection a particular science.

3

When an empirical material forms the basis of this connection, a material of which the connection constitutes a merely summarizing universality, the science is of a more *historical* kind. But if the Universal in the form of fundamental determinations and concepts precedes it and the particular element is supposed to be deduced from it, then the science is of a more strictly *scientific* kind.

4

There are no absolute boundaries to the range of the known facts which are to form the special element of a science; for each universal or concrete subject matter can be divided into its species or parts and each such species can in turn be considered as the subject matter of a special science.

5

In the *usual* Encyclopaedia the sciences are taken up empirically just as we find them. In such an Encyclopaedia the sciences are supposed to be presented in their completeness and, moreover, in so doing to be brought into an order in which similars and things which are grouped under common definitions are compared on the basis of an analogous relationship.

6

But a **Philosophical Encyclopaedia** is the science of the necessary connection, one determined by the Concept, and of the philosophical origination of the fundamental concepts and principles of the sciences.

7

It is properly the exposition of the general content of philosophy, for what is based on reason in the sciences depends on philosophy. On the other hand what in them rests on arbitrary and external determinations or, as it is called, is positive and is prescribed, as well as the merely empirical, lies outside philosophy.

8

According to the way in which they are cognized the sciences are either empirical or purely rational. From an absolute point of view both kinds ought to have the same content. Scientific effort aims at raising what is merely empirically known to what is always true to the Concept, to make it rational and incorporate it into rational science.

9

The sciences are expanded partly in an empirical direction and partly in their rational aspect. The latter happens when prominence is given more and more to the essential element which is grasped under general points of view, and the merely empirical element is grasped conceptually. The rational expansion of the sciences is at the same time an expansion of philosophy itself.

10

The whole of science is divided into three main parts:

(1) **Logic**;
(2) **The Science of Nature**;
(3) **The Science of the Spirit**.

Logic is the science of the pure Concept and of the abstract Idea. Nature and Spirit constitute the reality of the Idea, the former as an *external* existence, the latter as *self-knowing*. (Or, the logical is the eternally simple essence within itself; **Nature** is this essence as externalized; **Spirit** is the return of the essence into itself from its externalization.)

11

The sciences of Nature and Spirit can be considered as *applied* science, as the system of the real or special sciences in distinction from pure science or Logic, because they are the system of pure science in the shape of Nature and Spirit.

FIRST PART
LOGIC

12

Logic is the science of the pure **Understanding** [*Verstand*] and pure **Reason** [*Vernunft*] of their particular determinations and laws. Logic accordingly has three aspects:

(1) The abstract or non-dialectical [Understanding] [*verständige*];
(2) The dialectical or negatively rational;
(3) The speculative or positively rational.

The Understanding stops short at concepts in their fixed determinateness and difference from one another; dialectic exhibits them in their transition and dissolution; speculation or Reason grasps their unity in their opposition or the positive in their dissolution and transition.

13

Understanding and Reason are herein usually taken in the subjective sense in so far as they belong, as thinking, to a self-consciousness, so that logic is a merely *formal* science which requires another content, an external matter, if something really true is to result.

14

Logic considers the content of Understanding and Reason in-and-for-themselves and the absolute concepts as the absolutely true ground of everything, or the intellectual and rational in so far as it is not merely a subjective [*bewusstes*] comprehension. Consequently logic is in its own self speculative philosophy, for the speculative way of considering things is nothing else but a consideration of the essence of things which is just as much the pure concept peculiar to Reason as the nature and the law of things.

15

Logic divides into three parts:

(1) **Ontological Logic**;
(2) **Subjective Logic**;
(3) **The Doctrine of the Idea**.

The first is the system of the pure concepts of [immediate] Being [or extant things] [*des Seienden*]; the second is the system of the pure concepts of the Universal; the third contains the concept of Science.

FIRST SECTION
ONTOLOGICAL LOGIC

Being

A Quality

Being

16

(1) The beginning of the science is the immediate, wholly indeterminate concept of **Being**. (2) This, in its contentlessness, is equivalent to **Nothing**. 'Nothing' as the thought of emptiness thus inverts [*umgekehrt*] itself into a being and, on account of its purity, is the same as Being. (3) Being and Nothing contain no difference but what is, is only the positing of them as differentiated and the vanishing of each in its opposite, that is, pure **Becoming**.

Determinate Being

17

But because in Becoming those previously posited only vanish, Becoming is their collapse into a quiescent singleness in which they are not nothing but also are not self-subsistent, rather they are sublated or moments. This unity is **Determinate Being**.

18

Determinate Being is:

(1) a Being in the concept of which there lies at the same time the non-being of itself as a reference to other or **Being-for-Other**;

(2) but in acordance with the moment of Being it has the side of not being the reference to another, but of being in-itself. As the concept which embraces both these determinations it is **Reality**.

19

The Real [*Reelle*], or Something, as distinct from other Reals is, in the first instance, indifferent to it since in its Other-being it is at the same time in itself. The difference of the Real is first explicit in **Limit** as the middle between them in which they as much are as are not.

20

They are (1) distinct from the Limit or from their difference which is their middle, outside of which they are something. But (2) the Limit belongs to them because it *is their limit*.

21

The Difference is thus (1) the Real's own Difference or its **Determinateness**. This implicit Determinateness is however also (2) an external Determinate Being or **Constitution**. Determinateness which is as much external as internal constitutes **Quality**.

Alteration

22

Constitution, or external Determinate Being, belongs as much to Something as it is alien to it or is its Other-being, hence its own Not-being. It is thus the inequality of itself with itself, whereby **Alteration** is posited.

23

Alteration is the negating of the negative which something has within it, and gives rise to **Being-for-Self**. In other words Determinateness as the internal difference which something has in its own self, is the reference of something in its difference only to itself, or it is for-itself.

B Quantity

Being-for-Self (Ideality)

24

Being-for-Self is (1) difference, but only from itself, or the reference not to an other but to itself. (2) But in so far as the difference contains within itself Other-being and the reference to it is negative, the other is *for* it but as excluded.

25

Being-for-Self is the numerical **One**. It is simple, related only to itself and its other is excluded. Its Other-being is **Plurality**.

26

The **Many** are each the same. They are therefore **One**. But the One is just as much a Plurality. For its exclusion [of others] is the positing of its opposite or its posits itself thereby as a Plurality. The former, Becoming, is **Attraction**, the latter is **Repulsion**.

27

Since the one Becoming is posited no less than the other, their truth is their being at rest, which is no less the self-externality of the One or the positing of itself as Plurality, **Discreteness**, as the relation of the Many as self-equal is their **Continuity**, pure **Quantity**.

Quantum

28

Quantity has the negativity of the One in it only as sublated, or because in the self-sameness of Being-for-Self Other-being is immediately not an Other, as an external limit or is a limit which is no limit. Quantity with this indifferent limit is **Quantum**.

29

Quantum is *extensive* Quantum and in so far is the limit to the moment of plurality of quantity; or it is *intensive* Quantum in so far as it is related to the moment of self-sameness or is in the determination of self-sameness.

30

Since negativity is an indifferent limit to Quantum, Being-for-Self or the absolute determination is a *beyond* for it. Every Quantum can be exceeded and another limit posited, which equally is not an immanent limit. This gives rise to the *progress to infinity* or the *spurious infinite*.

31

The absolute determination which was posited as a beyond, is however as Being-for-Self Quantity's own moment. Or the limit which is no limit is none other than the Other-being sublated in Being-for-Self. It is the determinateness, the positing of which is a self-determination: *qualitative* **Magnitude** [*Grösse*].

C Infinity

32

Qualitative Magnitude as a simple determination is in the first instance *specific* Magnitude but as a self-differentiating Self-Determining it is a specifying of Magnitudes which are at the same time specifically related to each other, having a qualitative relationship, or whose Quotient is their Ratio and which stand in a qualitative relation to each other. Since here not only are the Magnitudes sublated as finite, but their sublation itself is posited as their qualitative law, this is their true, [actually] present infinitude.

Essence

A Concept of Essence

33

The simple penetration of the quantitative or external determination and of the inner self-determining is **Essence**. As penetration of the self-determination and the indifferent determinateness, it has in itself the moments of **Essentiality** and **Inessentiality**. The Essential is what belongs to the self-determination but the Inessential is the moment of indifferent Determinate Being [*Daseins*].

34

Becoming, as the Becoming of Essence is, in the first instance, the Doing [*Tun*], a transition of Essence into the freedom of Determinate Being which however remains within itself.

35

In so far as the Doing is a difference of Essence from itself and Determinate Being or Determinateness thereby results, it is the positing of Doing.

B Proposition

36

The **Proposition** contains the moments of **Remaining-within-itself** [*Insichbliebens*] or **Self-Sameness** and of pure Differentiation. The former would be pure **Matter**, the other pure **Form**. But pure Form is the doing which remains within itself and therefore is that self-sameness which was called pure Matter and so conversely pure Matter is the differenceless Asunderness [*Aussereinander*] and not different from pure Form.

37

But Difference must no less be posited and the unity of Form and Self-Sameness, in contrast to the Being-within-Self, is in the form of external Determinate Being, what is usually called Matter. In so far as it is in the form of an internal being it is a **Content** but the Form is each of these determinations of difference.

38

(1) The simple Proposition is the **Maxim of Identity**, $A = A$. It is indifferent to its Matter. Its content has no determination or has no filling, hence the Form is a differenceless Self-Sameness.

39

(2) The **Maxim of Indifferent Diversity** posits indeterminate Distinctiveness and asserts that there are no two things which are completely alike.

40

(3) The **Maxim of Opposition** runs: A is either B or $-B$, *Positivity* and *Negativity*. Of the opposed predicates only one belongs to things and there is no third between them.

41

(4) The **Maxim of the Ground** expresses the accomplished return into itself of what was posited or the positing itself as the third in which the opposed determinations are sublated, and which, as the Simple, is the opposite determination to the grounded as the manifold Determinate Being.

C   Ground and Grounded

Whole and Parts

42

Essence, as Ground of Determinate Being without which Essence itself is not, is in the first place **Whole** and **Parts**. The Whole is the positing of its Parts and conversely consists of them. The two sides constitute one and the same thing. The Whole is equal to the Parts only as their togetherness, i.e. to the Whole, and the Parts are equal to the Whole as a divided whole, i.e. as Parts; in other words, both sides are indifferent to one another and the activity of the Whole as Form has Matter for its Condition.

Force and its Expression

43

But the Parts are parts only as posited by the Whole. This their connection is determinateness through the unity of the Ground. Or the Quality of Determinate Being is posited by the activity of the Ground as Form, and the matter of appearance is the Ground's own content. Hence it is **Force** which expresses itself.

44

Force is the self-positing of its Determinate Being as a specific Quality. According to the side that Determinate Being is still a Being-for-Other or an Externality it is, at the same time, free from it and does not cease to be when this its appearance vanishes. In accordance with this aspect Force, it is true, no longer has Matter, which is its content and to which it immanently belongs, for condition but it still has a soliciting activity towards it.

45

The soliciting activity is itself Force and before it can solicit must itself be solicited. Since the relation of the two activities is this reciprocal exchange of their determinations, each is the Ground of the activity, or the Expression of the other. With this arises the concept of Ground which is the Ground of its own activity and of the other which activates it.

Inner and Outer

46

Essence is the Ground of Determinate Being as spontaneous activity and in its existence there is nothing alien or nothing at all which has not been posited by the Ground itself. Hence Essence and its Determinate Being are the same. Each relates itself as Inner to itself as Outer, which exhibits only what is Inner.

47

As this relationship Ground is the Unconditioned, the Inner, the Unity of Matter as a quiescent self-sameness and of Form as unity of the antithesis. Ground exhibits itself in its Determinate Being as Matter in which its forces repose and as the antithesis and play of the spontaneous and reciprocally active forces. Essence has herewith become **Actuality**.

Actuality

48

Actuality is the self-subsistent relation. It has the moments of its Appearance or its Existence which is its relation to itself, and of its Possibility, as the *in-itself* or Essence of its Determinate Being. The Actual itself is the unity of its possibility and its existence.

Substance

49

The Actual is **Substance**. It is Essence which contains within itself the determinations of its Determinate Being as simple attributes and laws and posits these as an existent play or as its **Accidents**, the sublation of which is not a vanishing of Substance but its return into itself.

50

Substance is the *necessity* of its Accidents. These have in their free Determinate Being the relation of their nature to an other as an inner relation concealed in them and they appear to lose their self-subsistence through external Accidents and an alien power. But in truth this is only the restoration of the Whole which takes back again into itself the separation effected on them.

Cause

51

Substance enters into the relationship of **Causality**, in so far as it exhibits itself in the antithesis of Necessity. The freely acting absolute Cause is Substance not only as the initiator of movement whose activity begins within itself but which also has within itself the whole content which it produces and which as Effect obtains Determinate Being.

52

Hence this activity as regards the opposition between the activity and what is Effect is a transition into Opposites, but as regards Content is an identical transition.

Reciprocity

53

Substance is, therefore, as Cause active only on-and-within-itself and stands only in a **Reciprocal** relation with itself: it is the Universal.

SECOND SECTION
SUBJECTIVE LOGIC

Concept

54
The **Concept** is the totality of determinations gathered up into their simple unity.

55
It has the moments of **Universality**, **Particularity** and **Individuality**.

56
Universality is the Concept's immanent unity in the determination. Particularity is the negative as a simple determination which is pervaded by Universality, or it is a distinguishing mark. Individuality is the negative as pure self-relating negativity.

57
Individuality, as a self-relating and indeterminate negativity, contains determination as a property as an indifferent though not self-subsistent but sublated Determinate Being and is **Subject**.

Judgement

58
Judgement is the separation of the Subject from its determination or particularity and the reference of the Subject to the determination which is its Predicate. Subject and Predicate are related to one another as Individual and Particular or Universal or also as Particular and Universal.

59
Judgement expands the Subject to Universality and, at the same time, posits its bounds. The Predicate goes herewith beyond the Subject and, at the same time, is contained in it, or the Predicate is, at the same time, Particular and Universal.

Quality of the Judgement or Determination of the Predicate

60

In that the Judgement is the relation of the Predicate to the Subject, its content and expression is in the first instance this: the Individual is Universal; (1) **Positive Judgement**. (2) But the Individual is not Universal, **Negative Judgement**, but a Particular. (3) The Individual is not a Particular; **Infinite Judgement**. The outcome is that every determination, the Universal sphere too and hence the Predicate generally, is sublated.

Quantity of the Judgement or Determination of the Subject

61

The Infinite Judgement contains the Individual as Individual or as *this*, and we have: (1) the Judgement: 'This is so constituted', **Singular Judgement**. Since the Predicate at the same time also expresses something Universal about the Subject, the Judgement must read: (2) 'Some are so constituted', **Particular Judgement**, which directly implies the opposite Judgement, 'Some are not so constituted.' (3) This indefiniteness is sublated by the Judgement, '*Everything* is so constituted'; **Universal Judgement**.

Relation of the Judgement or Determination of the Relation

62

Through the Qualitative and Quantitative Judgement the Subject as well as the Predicate has been posited in every determination of the Concept. The Concept is thus *in-itself* or implicitly before us and the Judgement now contains a reference of what is to be judged *to* the Concept. This Judgement proper is **Categorical**. But because that reference of the Concept to what is judged is at first only an *inner* connection the Categorical Judgement is at the same time only *assertorical*.

63

The **Hypothetical Judgement**: 'if "**A**" is, then "**B**" is', simply states the connection without assertion of Determinate Being. Thus the Judgement is *problematic*.

64

The **Disjunctive Judgement**: '"**A**" is either "**B**" or "**C**" or "**D**"', contains in the Predicate Universality and its Particularization. The Subject as Universal is no less connected with these determinations as these also exclude one another and only one of them can belong to the Subject. This Judgement is *apodictic*.

Syllogism

65

The **Syllogism** is the exhibition of the Concept in its terms. In it Individuality, Particularity and Universality are not only distinguished as terms but also the extremes are united by the middle term which is their unity.

66

(1) The Syllogism is, in the first place, the uniting of Individuality and Universality by Particularity as the middle term. The meaning of this syllogism is:

(a) The Individual is through its determinateness a Universal or has existence in general;
(b) The Individual has through its immediate determinateness still another determinateness which the former includes within itself.

67

The form of this Syllogism **I–P–U** is the general rule of subsumption of a specific content under a universal determination. If, as in identical propositions, this is not more Universal as regards content than that of which it is directly predicated, yet it has the form of Universality as predicated in relation to the other as Subject.

68

In quantitative determinations the terms of the Syllogism have no relation of form to one another except that of equality. The mathematical Syllogism therefore runs: 'Things which are equal to a Third are equal to one another.'

69

Syllogisms, whatever position the terms contained in them may have are to be brought back to the above stated form which is the general rule of all Syllogisms.

70

In the Syllogism, considered with regard to its determinate moments, the middle term is Particularity, a determinateness, the plurality of which embraces the Individual as a concrete which therefore can also be united with other universal determinations which can reciprocally limit and even annul one another. Similarly the Particular is on its own account referable to other universal determinations. Conversely the Universal embraces other determinatenesses and therefore also other Individualities. Consequently the Individual and the Universal which are united here are a contingent content for one another.

71

In regard to the relation of the terms there are in the Syllogism two immediate relations or judgements, namely that of the Individual to the Particular and that of the Particular to the Universal, and a mediated relation, the Conclusion. Because only the mediated relation contains the unity of the terms united and thereby, as regards form, the necessity of their relation, the two immediate relations must likewise be exhibited as mediations. But if this is done by the same kind of Syllogism we have the progress to the *spurious infinite*, since each of such interpolated syllogisms has the same defect.

72

The immediate relations of the Individual to the Particular and of the Particular to the Universal must therefore first be mediated in accordance with the general form of the Syllogism but by another determinateness of the middle term.

(2) Accordingly the second general Syllogism is that the Particular is united with the Universal by *Individuality*. But the Individual as determinate existent must, in so far as it is to be a middle term, be **Allness**: Syllogism by **Induction**. Now because the existent Individual belongs to free contingency Induction cannot become complete and this Syllogism consequently remains to that extent imperfect and also contains no inner necessity.

73

But Individuality, as the middle term, in so far as it is the *universal* moment of the Concept unites the Particular and the Universal in a genuine manner. It is the negative unity in which, as a process and an activity, Particularity, as a differentiated manifoldness and condition of Determinate Being, has been united into a One and raised into a simple universal Unity or, conversely, the Universal has been Particularized and has entered into the manifoldness of Determinate Being.

74

(3) Finally, the relation of Individuality to Particularity must be mediated and for this the Universal is to hand: Syllogism of **Analogy**. In this Syllogism the middle term, in its relation to the extreme of Particularity, has the determination of Individuality and falls apart into an Individual and a Universal since what counts only for the Individual is taken universally. This Syllogism therefore contains strictly speaking four determinations (*quaterni terminorum*) and accordingly is defective.

75

But Universality, as the genuine middle term, is the inner nature [of the Concept] and the whole Concept, in which the negative unity, the Subjectivity as well as the Objectivity, the content and the Particularity of Determinate Being interpenetrate and which is the absolute Ground and Connection of Being-within-Self and Determinate Being.

76

The first Syllogism, **I–P–U**, of the mediation of Individuality and Universality through Particularity, *presupposes* the two following, by which both of its immediate relations are mediated. But, conversely, both of these reciprocally presuppose each other and the first as well. The immediate calls for mediation and proceeds only from it, just as, conversely, mediation proceeds from the immediate. Each syllogism constitutes a circle of reciprocal presupposition which, as a totality, binds itself to itself and in the simple mediation which equally is immediate gathers itself together in the middle point.

77

This totality of reciprocally self-presupposing mediation which therein is a simple Immediacy brings forth a Determinate Being which has that cause and its activity for its presupposition but, conversely, what is brought forth is just as much ground of the activity and of the bringing forth itself. This *mediation* is therefore neither a *transition* like the Becoming of Being generally, in which what passes over is lost in its opposite; nor a *bringing forth* like the *appearing* of the ground which only immediately is; or the *expression* of Force whose activity is conditioned; nor an *activity* like that of Cause whose activity vanishes in the Effect.

[End]

78

(A) **End**, closely considered, is the real and self-realizing Concept, both as a Whole and in its Parts the entire syllogism. It is, in the first instance as Subjectivity, the whole syllogism, namely: (1) the immediate in-itself existing [*seiende*] Universal, that is (2) self-determining or particularizing itself and (3) impelling itself to go out of itself into Determinate Being.

79

(B) The realization of the End is equally the whole syllogism. This mediation is: (1) the active End as effective cause, but (2) by a means which belongs partly to the subjective element by the activity of which the means is brought into connection with the End; and partly to existence or objectivity and by the activity is brought into connection with this objectivity; (3) the activity acts on the immediate existence and by its sublation gives itself a mediated, produced objectivity.

80

This, the **Realization** of the End, exhibits mediation through the Universal. It is an externality which, on one side, is a Product and, on the other side, is Ground of the productive activity. Thus in the Realized End what effects the result has just as much come out of itself and passed over into its opposite as it has also returned into itself from its mediating activity and in its Other-being has found only itself.

81

(C) In so far as the End as active Cause lets means and product fall apart in existence, so that the means does not have the End, or the product the activity, in-themselves, Purposiveness is merely *external* and it is altogether *relative*, in so far as the End itself is of a subordinate content and what is a means for the End has this relation only according to some one or other of its sides.

82

The End of something is what it is in-itself and in truth, or is its Concept; relative Purposiveness which has regard to only one or other determinateness of something does not therefore exhaust its Concept.

83

Inner Purposiveness is where something is in its own self reciprocally as much End as Means, i.e. is its own product, and this product is the productive agent itself. Such a One is **Own-End** [*Selbstzweck*].

THIRD SECTION
DOCTRINE OF THE IDEA

84

The Idea is the adequate Concept in which Objectivity and Subjectivity are equal or in which Determinate Being corresponds to the Concept as such. It embraces the genuine Life of the Self [*Selbstleben*]. The Idea is partly Life, partly Cognition, partly Science.

The Idea of Life

85

Life is the Idea in the element of Determinate Being. Through the unity of the Concept and Objectivity the living Organism is a Whole in which the parts exist not for themselves but only through and in the Whole: *organic Parts* in which Matter and Form are an inseparable unity.

86

Life has in it the universal moments which constitute just as many universal organic systems: (1) its universal simple Being-within-Self in its externality, **Sensibility**; (2) stimulation from outside and immediate reaction to it, **Irritability**; (3) return into itself of this action outwards, **Reproduction**.

87

As a self-realizing spontaneous movement Life is a threefold process:

(1) The **Organization** [or **Formation**] [*Gestaltung*] of the Individual in-itself;
(2) Its **Self-Preservation** in face of its inorganic nature;
(3) The **Preservation of the Species**.

88

The process of **Organization** is the relation of the Organism to itself and consists in all the organic parts reciprocally and continuously producing themselves, the maintenance of one part depending on the maintenance of the others. This production is partly only a development [*Evolution*] of the implicitly already existing organization, partly the perpetual alteration of it. Mere **Growth** or quantitative alteration is however a process of increase by **Intussusception** not by juxtaposition, i.e. not a mechanical increase.

89

The process of *organic* **Alteration** is just as little a chemical process. In Chemism two related materials are indeed oppositionally expressed [*aufeinander bezogen*] through their Concept (chemical affinity) and therefore contain *in principle* [*an sich*] their Product which is not already produced by what is previously to hand and equivalent to it. But its production is not a Self-Preservation of itself. It is therefore only a neutral product, i.e. one in which the activity which belongs only to the separate matters is extinguished, is not self-productive, and is separable again into its constituents in regard to quality and quantity.

90

The organic **Nutritive Process** is, on the other hand, a complete determination of the material increase by the inner already existing Form which as the Subjective, or as the simple Form of all Parts, relates itself to itself, each part bearing itself towards the others as towards something Objective, and is only with itself in the process.

91

The **Self-Preservation Process** of the Organism opposed to its inorganic nature. – The free opposition of Life into Subjective and Objective presents itself as an organic and an inorganic nature. The latter is Life without Individuality in which the Individual exists for-itself, possessing its concept only as a law of Nature's necessity [and] not in a subjective form and its meaning falling only in the Whole. This Whole, as Subject, is the Organism to which inorganic Nature is essentially related, constituting therein the Organism's condition.

92

The inorganic **Condition** is related to the Organism not as cause or as a chemical moment, but on the contrary, what is posited in the Organism by the action on it of the inorganic is essentially determined by the Organism itself and acts only as a *stimulus*. The Organism is the double movement of the perpetual struggle which, on the one hand, checks the process of the elements and their transition into opposites, annuls its condition and Individualizes the objective universality, but, on the other hand, discharges from itself what is Individual or Subjective and deposes it to an inorganic existence.

93

The process of the **Preservation of the Species** is: (1) the realization of the species generally which, as a universal Life, passes over into Individuality by particularizing the species to an actuality in the Individual; (2) the relation of the Organism to a similar Organism whereby it produces itself as another Individual of the same species. The preservation of the species is exhibited in this exchange of Individuals and in the return of Individuality to Universality.

The Idea of Cognition

94

Cognition is the exhibition of an object according to its existent determinations as these are grasped in the unity of its Concept and are yielded by it, or conversely, in so far as the Concept's own activity gives it its determinations. These determinations, posited as contained in the Concept, are Cognition, or the Idea realizing itself in the element of Thought.

The Idea of Knowing

95

Knowing has (1) for its object nothing external, nothing in any way given but itself alone. It is the Concept existing as Concept. (2) The Concept construes itself from itself in that it is a process and exhibits the opposition contained in it in the form of various self-subsistent real determinations or determinations of the Understanding. (3) Since the real determinations become at first, in their reflection, determinations of the Understanding, their dialectic exhibits them not only as essentially relating themselves to one another but also as passing over into their unity. Out of this their negative movement there results their positive unity which constitutes the Concept in its real totality.

SECOND PART
SCIENCE OF NATURE

96
Nature is the absolute Idea in the shape of Other-being as such, of indifferent, external Objectivity and of the concrete individualized actualization of its moments; or it is absolute Being in the determination of immediacy as such in contrast to its mediation. The Becoming of Nature is the Becoming of Spirit.

97
Nature is to be regarded as a system of grades of which one arises necessarily from the other but not in such a way that one is generated by the other naturally but rather in the inner Idea lying at the base of Nature. The movement of the Idea of Nature is to withdraw into itself from its immediacy, to sublate itself and to become Spirit.

98
The Science of Nature considers (1) the ideal existence [*Dasein*] of Nature as Space and Time generally, (2) as Inorganic Nature, (3) [as] Organic Nature and is accordingly;

(1) **Mathematics**;
(2) **Physics of the Inorganic**;
(3) **Science of Organic Nature**.

FIRST SECTION
MATHEMATICS

99
Space and **Time** are the existent abstractions, or the pure Form, pure Intuition of Nature. Space is the existent thought of universal indifferent diversity in general; Time is the existent thought of negative unity or of pure Becoming.

100
Space and Time are Infinite, i.e in the abstract continuity of their self-externality, *boundless*. But as Ideas, they have within themselves the determinations which exhibit the concept in its moments: the **Dimensions**.

101

(1) The **Dimensions of Space** are its moments, which are not asunder but where one is, each of the others is also. They are also indeed formal differences: the one, the other and the third as unity of them. But owing to the qualityless unity of Space they are not determined in opposition to one another but are empty differences which only acquire an alien determinateness in respect of a further object.

102

(2) The Dimensions of Time are:

(a) The **Past**, existence as sublated, as non-existent;
(b) The **Future**, the non-existent but destined to exist;
(c) The **Present**, as the immediate Becoming and union of both.

103

Because Space is in the determination of a real indifferent determinate existence real bounds appear in it and its dimensions, which at first are only mere **Directions** as such constituting the *forms* of this its **Limitation**.

104

To the limitation of Space belongs only the indifferent determination of quantity. *Continuous* Magnitude, which at first is the kind of its quantity as such, is itself an indeterminate determination. Absolute determinateness lies in *discrete* Magnitude, the principle of which is the **One**.

105

Space is the object of a (synthetic) science, **Geometry**. This is because in Geometry as such the continuous quantum can be visibly represented and because in it, as in the element of indifferent sundered manifoldness which, however, is, at the same time, continuous, the concept of an object expresses itself in a real shape in which more is contained than the essential determination of the Concept.

106

Time, however, as such is incapable of being a complete schema or **Figure of Quantum**. As a restless Becoming it is not an element of a synthetic whole. In becoming a quantity it passes over into the negative determination of Quantity, into the unit, which is the principle for an [analytical] science of Quantity, **Arithmetic**. This is because the units are not combined in accordance with an elementary intuition of reality itself but the combination is one imposed upon them.

107

In Arithmetic and Geometry quanta are compared with each other however arbitrary and general their magnitudes may be, yet in accordance with this determination, belonging to them so far as they are not in relation, they count as complete or independently determined quanta, as *finite Magnitudes*. The *analysis* of the Infinite, but chiefly the differential and integral calculus, treat of *infinite Magnitudes*, i.e. such as no longer have the significance of finite or independently and completely determined magnitudes but are vanishing magnitudes which have their value only in their *final Ratio* or at *their Limit*, i.e. solely in the Ratio.

108

The **Differential Calculus** finds for a formula the expression of the final ratio of its variable finite magnitudes. Conversely the **Integral Calculus** seeks the finite expression for formulae which contain final ratios.

109

Applied Mathematics applies *pure* Mathematics to the quantitative relationships of Nature which it takes from experience.

SECOND SECTION
PHYSICS

Mechanics

110

Pure Intuition which has passed over from its immediacy into being-in-and-for-itself, or into filled space and time, is **Matter**. The asunderness of space and the being-within-self of time posited absolutely in one, yield the concept of Matter in general.

111

According to the moment of being-within-self Matter would be a single isolated point; according to the moment of self-externality it would be in the first place a host of mutually excluding **Atoms**. But since these, in excluding one another, are no less mutually related the

Atom has no actuality and the Atom, like absolute continuity or infinite divisibility, is only a possibility in Matter.

112

Matter, as existing on its own account, has the moment of Individualization but it no less maintains itself in being-in-itself and is only an essential continuity, **Heaviness**. This constitutes the universal predicate of a body which is Matter in the form of Subject.

113

Body contains the connections of the ideal moments of space and time, which connection appears as **Motion** and Heaviness as their ground.

114

Free motion belongs to bodies which possess their own *centre* of heaviness. Through the relation of such centres arises the free system of the *circular* motion of the celestial bodies, whereas on the other hand, other bodies lacking a centre of their own lack centrifugal force and are subject to centripetal force whereby they *fall*.

115

In the magnitude of Motion besides space and time mass is a moment, and just as space and time also pass over into Force they are, like Mass, moments of Force.

Physics of the Inorganic

116

Heaviness, which is individualized by light and opened up into qualitative differences, is concrete or physical Nature and the object of Physics generally.

117

Heaviness is the opposite to the being-within-self towards which self-externality only *strives*. Matter is this existence of the effort whose opposition expresses itself only in the moments of space and time, in a merely ideal centre. That process of self-externality towards a being-within-self, the intensive simple unity of heaviness, is an existence confronting it, the freely existing self of matter, **Light**. Light as a self-equal being-within-self is the principle of the individualizing and particularity of matters. Its relation to what is merely negative to it, to darkness, it constitutes **Colour**.

118

The first moment of the particular existence of physical Nature is **Magnetism**, the diremption of the individual point of unity into opposition which, however, remains still enclosed within the concept.

119

The second moment is the realization, that is, the liberating and self-constituting of the sides of the opposition (1) as **Electricity**, which is the still unembodied fleeting manifestation of the opposition, the sides of which are held in absolute tension against each other; (2) [as] the **Chemical Elemental Matters**. They are the qualitative differences of corporeity in the shape of special matters which however are still abstract and without an actual individuality. (3) The **Physical Bodies**, in which the qualitative determinations are in a concrete corporeity, which though containing within themselves all the moments of corporeity, but under the determination of one of these moments or qualities, assume the shape of an indifferent subsistence towards one another:

(a) As the **Physical Elements**, air, water, fire, earth.
(b) As absolute or **Celestial Bodies**, and
(c) As **Terrestrial Bodies** which have passed on into a further distribution and particularization.

120

The third moment is the **Chemical Process**. The particularization of bodies and their own indifferent independent existence is at the same time a relation of them to one another, not only a reciprocal tension but also an opposition whereby their indifferent subsistence is annulled and brought back into the unity of totality. But this returning process coincides in living Nature with the process of construction whereby the union at the same time from another side becomes a secretion and precipitation of an indifferent existence.

THIRD SECTION
PHYSICS OF ORGANIC NATURE

121

Geology treats of the formations of the earth as the result of the extinct process of the formation of the earth-Individual. Geognosy considers these formations in their generality as rocks according to their constitution and stratification, and together with **Oryctog-**

nosy, which treats principally of the separate formations as constituent parts of those general formations and veins or lodes, constitutes **Mineralogy**.

122

Vegetable Nature is the beginning of the incipient individual or subjective process of self-preservation or the organic process proper. This, however, does not yet possess the complete force of individual unity in that the plant which is a *single* Individual possesses only such parts which can in turn be regarded as independent individuals. Because the plant lacks this inner unity it does not develop feeling. **Plant Physiology** considers the general nature of plant life but **Botany** treats of the system of the plant and bases its classification mainly upon the differences between the organs of fertilization, which latter forms the apex of plant life by which plants border on a higher stage of the organism.

123

Animal Nature possesses that subjective unity whereby every organic part is subordinated to a whole which is a One. The **Physiology** of the animal organism treats of the functions of the parts which cooperate in the perpetual production of the whole and which through this process are themselves produced and preserved. **Comparative Anatomy** considers the general *types* of the animal in the different forms of the universal species, partly how the type begins to show itself in the simplest animal organisms and gradually appears in a more developed form, and partly how it is modified in accordance with the various elements in which animal species appear. **Zoology** classifies these in the first place according to their common distinct characteristics and for this purpose takes the determinations from the main stages of the development of the animal types, from the element [in which it lives], and finally from its weapons in relation to other organisms. But in all this Nature effaces the specific bounds which here offer themselves, by the transitions which unite one principle with another.

124

The organism in accordance with the moment of its irritability stands generally in a relation with its inorganic nature. This disunion is at first subjectively present in it as a feeling of lack, as a *need*. This subjective disunion is reflected outwards in the opposition between Organic and Inorganic Nature. The *inorganic powers* [*Potenzen*] behave as a stimulus to the Organism whose activity is the perpetual struggle to take them up into itself according to its receptivity and therein to be victorious, thereby restoring the unity within itself, which unity is itself a similar process of the opposition of the internal systems to one another and a restoration of them.

125

The organism is in the state of **Disease** when it cannot overcome one of the powers [*Potenzen*] posited in it, the power fixing itself in a system which isolates itself, perseveres in its own activity and no longer passes over into the fluid activity of the whole. The organic process is thus converted into one that is interrupted. The science of Disease and its cure is **Medicine**.

126

The animal has *feeling* in so far as its organic moments have their determination and meaning only and solely in the unity of life, but at the same time they still have an external asunderness. The final reflection of this externality into the abstract element of simplicity [of oneness], which alone constitutes the complete subsistence of the moments, is the elevation into Spirit.

THIRD PART
SCIENCE OF SPIRIT

127

Spirit only begins from the outer world, determines this, and henceforth is related only to itself and to its own determinations.

128

The Philosophy of Spirit contains three sections. It considers:

(1) **Spirit in its Concept**, Psychology in general;
(2) **The Realization of Spirit**;
(3) **The Consummation of Spirit in Art, Religion and Science** [or **Philosophy**].

FIRST SECTION
SPIRIT IN ITS CONCEPT

129

Spirit considered on its own is to be comprehended:

(1) In its *natural existence* [*natürlichen Dasein*] and in its direct connection with the organic body and its consequent dependence on the body's affections and states: **Anthropology**;
(2) As manifested, that is, in so far as it is related as subject to an other as object, Spirit is *consciousness* and the object of the **Phenomenology of Spirit**;
(3) As Spirit in accordance with the determinations of its activity within itself it is the object of **Psychology**.

130

Intelligence begins from externality as its *condition* but not as its principle; it is on the contrary itself the principle. It is (1) immediate as **Feeling**, the content of which (2) it raises to **Representation** or **Pictorial Thinking** within itself and (3) as **Thinking** it purifies the content of the contingency and particularity of its determinations and raises them to necessity and universality.

Feeling

131

Feeling is the simple but none the less specific affection of the individual subject in which no difference of the subject from the object has been posited, or it is a determination posited in the subject which is not yet separated from the object.

132

Feeling is partly inner, partly outer and is immediate, still without any reflection and as a Mood is either pleasant or unpleasant.

Representation

133

Feeling is the original stuff still self-enwrapped which intelligence raises to **Representation** by setting aside the form of simple oneness which feeling has and dividing it into an objective, and a subjective which separates itself from it, thus making Feeling into *something felt*.

134

It is first in Representation that we have an **Object**. The stages in forming Representations are that Intelligence:

(1) *Inwardizes* [recollects] itself, in that it completely separates itself

from the content of Feeling;
(2) *Imagines* this content, retains it without its object, freely evokes it from itself and connects itself with it;
(3) Takes away the immediate meaning of the content and gives it another meaning and association in **Memory**.

A   Recollection

135

1. **Intuition** is immediate Representation in which the determinations of Feeling are made into an object separated from the subject and which is free from the individual subject and, at the same time, is for it. But it is just as much not *for* the subject as a single individual but *for* everyone.

136

The **Object** thus posited as outside the subject and in its own self as an externality is partly the quiescent side-by-sideness of space, partly a restless becoming in the successive moments of time. Space and time are abstract intuitions or *Universal Forms of Intuition*.

137

In these universal objective elements the object, besides having the content of the determinations of feeling, is at the same time a single object completely determined in space and time and connected with other objects *before*, *alongside* and *after*. (Through this determinateness in space and time and through one another according to their determinations, things are caught and in the universal prison.)

138

2. **Representation**. Feeling becomes objective in Intuition. The subject is in immediate relation to Intuition and submerged in it so that in Intuition it has strictly speaking no other being than that objective, spatial and temporal being. The voluntary activity of intelligence consists here in **Attention** to the manifold existence of what is present and in the **Arbitrariness** [*Willkür*] of staying with a content or passing on to another: **Perceptive Faculty**.

139

But Intuition, as Object, is at the same time *for the subject*. This latter as being-in-and-for-itself withdraws itself from its self-externality, reflects itself into itself, and separates itself from objectivity in that it makes the intuition subjectively into an **Image** [*Bild*].

140

Intuition transposed into the **I [Ego]**, is not only Image but becomes Representation generally. The ego does not stop short at the intuition which has been internalized corresponding completely to the immediate intuition but the intuition is liberated from and taken out of its context in space and time. It is *sublated*, i.e. just as much a *non-existent* as a *preserved* existence.

141

Intuition as Representation is the subject's *own* time and space, transported into Time and Space as *universal forms*. Through the sublation of the particular time of Intuition it becomes *enduring*; through its own particular space it is *everywhere*.

142

Furthermore concrete Intuition is preserved in its manifold determinations or in their unity but equally it is also liberated from the bond of their singularity. The determinations of the parts fall asunder and become abstractions which are represented as *subsisting for themselves* without the sensuous context in which they at first appeared to the subject.

143

3. **Recollection**: Recollection as the inwardized Intuition or the Intuition made universal is related to immediate Intuition as a permanent and universal to the singular. Recollection in not so much comparison of the single intuition as the subsumption of the present single intuition under the already made universal or representation. The *sameness* which I recognize is, on the one hand, the identity of their content and, on the other, I recognize in the present intuition my own identity with myself or I remember *myself* in it.

144

The Image or Representation is not made a universal by the fact that the same intuition would be often repeated and the numerous intuitions would collapse into a single image either consciously, or our remembering with each single intuition the previous one; on the contrary, the intuition acquires immediately the form of universality by my acceptance of it. It is therefore a *subsumption*. In Recollection it is by a present intuition or representation that the image of a *former* one is evoked which was identical with the *present* one. The previous one is the permanent and universal under which I subsume the present single representation.

B Imagination

145

In Recollection the former and the present intuitions directly coincide. I am not faced by two different things, Intuition and Representation. It is only that I have had them and that they are already *mine*. In so far as I now also have before me the Representation as *different* from the Intuition, this is **Imagination**. For in the Imagination Intuition and Representation can be entirely different.

146

(1) *Reproduction* of Representation generally. Imagination as reproduction of a Representation generally evokes again the images and representations *without* the present intuition corresponding to them and lets them enter into consciousness on *their own account*.

147

(2) As *active*, Imagination brings the preserved images and representations into a manifold connection with one another which differs from that which they had as intuitions.

148

This connection can take place according to the various determinations which the representations contain. The various modes of connection have *very inappropriately* been called *laws of the association of ideas*.

149

The determination of the combination can be a more or less superficial or fundamental connection: mere contemporaneity or the same place of two representations, or any kind of Similarity or also Contrast of them; relations of *Whole* and *Parts*, *Cause* and *Effect*, *Ground* and *Consequent*, etc., generally any kind of sensuous or mental connection. The connection is dominated by an interest of the feeling, of a passion, or of the mental character generally.

150

The distinction between Images and Intuitions has already been stated. It is made by the ordinary consciousness directly in the waking and healthy state. But in sleep, in unusual states, in illness, this distinction falls away and imagination dominates it in face of intuition and superior mental powers.

151

(a) **Dreaming**: In Dreaming sleep we experience a range of representations indistinguishable from intuitions which are occasioned by memories or even by present sensations but besides are mixed up with and fastened on to the most contingent and arbitrary things. It is true that profounder interest or forces than mere imagination underlie *premonitions, visions, reveries*, etc., but they are linked with a particular heightening of the imagination which turns inner, obscurer feelings into pictures and gives them the intensity of intuitions.

(Sympathy with Nature. So-called Prevision. The future sleeps in the actual present. The actual present is at the same time possibility of what is to come. Oracles, prophesying from the flight of birds, from the entrails of animals. Universal mood stemming from Nature, like animals having presentiments of earthquakes. Races who live more in unity with Nature have a closer connection with it than we who have torn ourselves loose from Nature. Inner light; dealing with higher spirits; witches ointment of hyoscyamus; witches stupefied themselves and fell into a frightful fantasy which became epidemic. Thousands of them were burnt. Ghosts; often occasioned by external phenomena in which fantasy takes hold. The bad conscience racked by the torment of crime objectifies itself by ghostly shapes. Appointments to appear in life after death. Irrational enthusiasum, Fanaticism, esteeming religious ideas [*Vorstellungen*] higher than everything ethical in life, and than the relationship determined by the Concept. Irrational enthusiasm falls into the error of regarding an unimaged appearance as inferior to the tangible outer world. The world of sense is supposed to rank above the spiritual. The absolute is supposed to be present in the outer world. One wants to see God in a thing, without the medium of art; or one wants to bring the absolute Being to one's inner intuition, before one's imagination; *one wants to bring God down into the world of time and sense*. Genuine ascendancy of representation over intuition by the will, e.g. Mucius Scavola).

152

(b) A higher stage of the life which surrounds itself with fantasy is **Somnambulism**, sleep-walking proper, or other similar states, in which the mind, with a weaker or stronger outer perception, has a mere inner intuition of the outer world and is altogether active *within itself* and proceeds to a whole series of external arrangements as one does in the waking state.

(Somnambulism is:

(i) The usual kind in *sleep*: hearing music, reading, letter writing, going to dangerous places; bath-tub in front of the bed; intense shivering;
(ii) The *epilectic* kind: reading by the finger on the stomach, etc.;
(iii) The *magnetic* [hypnotic] sort; the patient answers only him who is *en rapport* with him.)

153

(c) Apart from the fact that **Raving in Delirium** is a state similar to and dependent on illness, insanity has various modifications, such as madness proper, mania, raving, etc. and is in general a domination of fantasies in the waking state over intuitions and intellectual ideas. *Madness proper* has some single fixed crazy idea which is correctly bound up with the rest of ideas in the fixed idea. *Mania* is a general breakdown of the mental faculties. This madness in the form of *frenzy* or *raving* is associated with a malicious spiteful will and outbreaks of rage.

(Imagining that one is a king, a cardinal, a person in the godhead. Melancholy arising from an idea of moral worthlessness. Someone believes that when he urinates he floods a whole town; another that he is a grain of barley and the chickens will eat him; a third that his feet are made of glass and he has a little bell in his stomach, and so on. The causes are:

(i) *Physical*; often a natural inherited disposition, impressions at the time of pregnancy; debauchery; poisonous herbs; rabies; diseased matter which acts on the nerves, brain etc.;
(ii) *Mental*; an extremely vivid idea, e.g. people have not only died from joy but have become insane; derangement through passions, love, pride, hope, vanity, disappointment; distrust destroys the connection with the outer world. The life of the lunatic is buried within himself, in his individuality; and so on. Accordingly the mode of cure of psychological disturbances is both physical and mental.)

[*Productive Imagination*]

154

The superior imagination, the poetic fantasy, does not serve contingent states and determinations of the feelings but Ideas and the truth of spirit generally. It strips off the contingent and arbitrary circumstances of existence, draws out what is inner and essential in them, shapes them and represents them in an image or symbol. This form of phenomenal existence which it gives to it is borne, dominated, permeated and bound into a unity only by its essential core. The symbolizing activity of the imagination consists in inserting beneath sensuous phenomena or images, conceptions or thoughts of a *different* kind from those immediately expressed, which nevertheless have an *analagous* relation to them and exhibit those images as the expression of them.

(Poetry is not an imitating of Nature. It is true in a higher sense, than ordinary actuality. The poet is a profound spirit whose penetrating vision sees in substance what another person also possesses in himself but does not become conscious of. It is true also here that no man is a hero to his valet. What this means is that, 'Yes I too have known him but have not seen anything heroic in him'; or 'I too have known love but have not found anything in it that the poet talks about'. The poet is for this reason a seer. The poet unites the splendour of Nature into a whole as the attributes of something higher; celestial blue is its garment, blossoms its messenger, and so on, Ceres and Proserpine. Basis of the Idea, Summer: Forget-me-nots, Sunrise: 'Thus sprang forth the sun, as rest springs forth from virtue,' Sunset: 'Thus dies a hero.' Symbolism of bread and wine in the Eleusinian mysteries and in Christianity. A deep disposition generally symbolizes; tendency of the Germans to think poetically of Nature.)

C Memory

155

(1) The **Sign**, in general. Representation, being liberated from outer existence and made subjective, the outer existence and the inner representation stand opposed to each other as different. The *arbitrary association* of an outer existence with a representation that does not correspond to it but, as regards content, is also different from it so that the outer existence [which] is to be the Representation, or the *meaning* of the Representation, makes the outer existence into a Sign.

156

Productive Memory, therefore, produces the association of Intuition and Representation, but a *free* association in which the preceding relation, in which Intuition forms the basis of Representation, is *reversed*. In the association of Reproductive Memory sensuous existence has no value on its own account but only the value given to it by Spirit.

157

Through its determinations sensuous existence is generally connected with another existence. But since its determination is a representation made by Reproductive Memory or *Mnemosyne* it becomes, to that extent, a connection of representations to other thinking beings and therein begins the theoretical communication of these with one another.

158

(2) **Language**. The highest work of the Reproductive Memory is Language, which is partly vocal and partly written. But, since Reproductive Memory is its source, we can talk of a further source only with regard to the invention of specific Signs.

159

Sound is the fleeting manipulation of something inner which in this utterance does not remain an outer but announces itself as something subjective and inner which essentially has a meaning. It is of particular importance that by the *articulation of sounds* not only can pictures [and] images be indicated but even *abstract ideas* [*Vorstellungen*]. The Concrete Idea is, in general, converted by the *word-sign* into something *unpictured* that is identified with the sign.

(The image is killed and the word takes the place of the image. This is a lion; *the name passes for the thing*. Logos; God spake, etc., Language is the highest power possessed by mankind. Adam, it is said, gave to everything (animals) its name. Language is the destruction [*Ertötung*] of the sensuous world in its immediate existence, the sublating of it into an existence which is a summons that echoes in every thinking being.)

160

With regard to the invention of specific signs it is natural for *sound phenomena* [for example] rustling, humming, buzzing, etc., that direct imitations of them are made. For other sensuous objects or changes the sign is on the whole arbitrary. For designating more abstract relationships and determinations symbols are used. The further development of language belongs to the power of universality, to the Understanding.

161
Written Language is *hieroglyphic* or *alphabetic*. The former is a designation of objects which has no relation to their sound sign. The idea of a universal philosophical written language proposed by some is impracticable because of the innumerable host of signs which would be necessary and, especially, to invent and to learn them. *Alphabetical* written language dissolves the word-signs into their simple sounds and designates them.

162
Reproductive Memory. This is the retention of individual signs in relation to what they designate, and principally the retention of an unimaged series of them which are not linked together by imaged or intellectual connection but are in a completely arbitrary or contingent sequence and are held together in this way by a purely inner, independent force.

Thinking

163
Thinking is Spirit's activity in its independent self-same simplicity which posits *from* and *within itself* determinations which have the character of self-sameness and universality.

1 Understanding

164
The **Understanding** is principally a thinking determination [of objects] and a holding fast to the thought determinations. As **Objective Understanding** it contains the Categories, the thought determinations of Being which constitute the inner unity of the manifold of intuitions and representations. It distinguishes the essential from the inessential and apprehends the necessity and *laws* of things.

2 Judgement

165
Judgement is a *relating* of an Individual to the Concept. It determines the Individual in a general way, or *subsumes* it under the Universal. It has the following stages.

166
(a) It is the Universal as [that by] which the Individual is determined, but is itself only some one *quality* of it, of which it has several.

167
(b) **Reflection** is to go beyond a single determination, to compare it with others and to combine them in a specific determination. The Universal constitutes the inner nature and essence of the object. This Universality is not merely a common property of the determinations but a Universality belonging to the object itself in contrast to the determinations of its own Particularity or Individuality.

168
(c) The Judging of an object is strictly speaking the comparison of its nature or true Universality with its Individuality, or with the constitution of its existence; the comparing of what it is with what it is supposed to be.

(In this Judging lies the dialectic that what is bad does not correspond to its concept but is, at the same time, also appropriate to it. A bad house has an existence which does not conform to its concept. But if it did not conform to it at all it would not be a house. The concept must still be recognisable in the existence. Thus if an action is judged to be bad, its un-Reason has all the same a side on which it is in agreement with Reason and so on.)

169
Mention can be made here of **Perspicacity** which refers more to the nature of one's Judgement than it is an actual stage of Judgement. It consists mainly in grasping distinctions which do not lie on the surface and by reflection to notice finer or deeper connections. **Wit** links ideas which, looked at superficially, are alien to one another but from another aspect present an unexpected similarity. **Ingenuity**, Cleverness, is an analogue to rationality and mainly expresses a determination or relationship which, in its immediate representation or in its own self, is opposed to itself.

3 Rational Thinking

170
(a) **Reason** is *negative* or *dialectical* when it points out the transition into its opposite of a determination of Being by the Understanding. Generally, dialectic appears when two opposite predicates are

asserted of a single subject. The purer form of dialectic consists in showing that a determination of a predicate by the Understanding is *in its own self* just as much the *opposite of itself*, that it, therefore, sublates itself within itself.

171

(b) **Ratiocinative Reason** seeks the *grounds* of things; i.e. of their being posited by and in an other which is their essence. But this essence, which remains enclosed within itself, is, at the same time, only *relatively unconditioned*, since what is grounded or is a consequent has a content other than the ground.

172

(c) **Syllogistic Reason** contains the mediation of a content which stands in the relationship of the determinations of the Concept, as Individual, Particular, and Universal. The Particular is related to the Individual as a Universal and, in relation to the Universal, is a specific [Particular]; it is the middle term which contains within itself the extremes of Individuality and Universality and thus links them together.

Syllogistic reason is:

(i) **Formal Reason** in so far as the Syllogism is subjective. What appears in it as mediated or as a consequent is in itself the immediate. It has the relationship of something mediated only for cognition.
(ii) **Teleological Reason** considers and posits ends, a relationship in which what is mediated or brought forth has the same content as the immediate, the presupposed Concept, and in which what is mediated, the consequent, is just as much ground.
(iii) **The Idea of Reason** is the Concept in that its externality or reality is completely determined by it and exists only in its Concept; in other words, the existent [thing] which has in it its own Concept is the means of itself; the means, therefore, is just as much end.

SECOND SECTION
PRACTICAL SPIRIT

173

Practical Spirit not only *has* Ideas but *is* the living Idea itself. It is Spirit that determines itself from its own resources and gives its determinations an external reality. A distinction is to be made between the 'I' as only theoretical or ideal and the 'I' which practically or really makes itself into an object, into an objectivity.

174
Practical Spirit means especially *free will* in so far as the 'I' can abstract from every determinateness in which it is placed and remains undetermined and self-equal in every determinateness.

175
The Will, as the self-determining Concept, is essentially *activity* and *action*. It translates its inner determinations into outer existence in order to exhibit itself as Idea.

176
To the **Deed** there belongs the whole range of determinations which are immediately connected with the resultant alteration of an existence. To the **Action** there belongs in the first place only that part of it which was in the **Resolve** or in consciousness. It is consciousness alone that acknowledges Will as its own and that bears the blame which can properly be imputed to it. But, in a wider sense, blame can also be imputed in respect of those determinations of the action of which the doer was not conscious but *could* have been conscious.

177
(a) **Practical Feeling** does include the practical legal and moral determinations and laws, but only immediately, so that they are undeveloped and not thought out and on the whole are *impure* through the admixture of a subjective individuality. It is essential to notice that Practical Feeling has no other genuine content than the rights, duties and laws which are specifically known; that, on the one hand, it is obscure and determined by individuality and, on the other hand, can be given precedence over the specific consciousness of them only in so far as they are adhered to *separately* and consciousness can oppose itself to them as a totality.

178
(b) The feeling of a practical determination associated with the feeling of its contradiction, of being only inner and unrealized, for which however, reality is at the same time essential, this is **Impulse**. It belongs to the subjective nature and is directed only to its determinateness. **Appetite** is a *single* determination of Impulse, and

Feeling becomes pleasant or unpleasant according to whether external existence is conformable to it or not. In Impulse and Appetite, Practical Spirit is, in its natural existence, a dependent unfree being.

179
(c) Spirit must raise itself out of its submergence in Impulse to Universality so that Impulses, in their separateness, do not possess absolute validity; on the contrary their determinations receive their place and correct value only as *moments of the totality* whereby they are purged of subjective contingency.

180
The determinations of Spirit constitute its laws. However, they are not external or natural determinations of it. The *sole* determination in which *all* are contained is its *Freedom*, which is both the form and content of its law which can be *Legal*, *Moral* or *Practical*.

Law

181
Spirit as a free self-conscious being is the self-equal 'I' which in its absolutely negative relation is in the first place an exclusive 'I', an individual free being or **Person**.

182
Law is the relationship between people in so far as they are abstract Persons. An action is *illegal* by which someone is not respected as a Person or which encroaches on the sphere of his freedom. This relationship is therefore, in accordance with its fundamental determination, of a *negative* nature and does not strictly demand the proof to the other person of anything positive but only that he himself be left alone as a Person.

183
The external sphere of Law and Freedom constitutes **Property**, the subsumption of something unowned under my power and my will. **Possession** is the side of arbitrarily *taking possession*. The aspect of Property as such a Possession is the universal side, that Possession is an expression of my will, which as something Absolute, must be respected by others.

184

I can **Dispose** of my Property, of what is in fact Property, i.e. what partly is *mine*, partly has within itself the moment of *externality*. What is inalienable from me is my reason, my freedom, my personality and altogether what essentially contains within it my *entire* freedom.

185

I can alienate my Property to another and can acquire Property which is *not* mine. This acquisition takes place only by **Contract**: the mutual consent of two persons to alienate a property and to let it pass to another and the consent of the other to accept it.

186

The sphere of my freedom contains my Personality and the relation of something to this. When this sphere is violated by another this can happen either in the sense that only this thing does not belong to me, so that my Personality itself is recognized; or in the sense that my personality itself is not recognized, which is the case when my body and life suffer injury.

187

In injuring my Personality the other directly injures his own. What he does to me is not something merely individual but something universal. What, according to the concept, he has done to himself, must be made an actuality. When this is done by the injured party it is **Revenge**; when it is carried out by the Universal Will, and in its name, it is **Punishment**.

188

Law in relation to Property constitutes the object of **Civil Law**. Law in relation to the Personality is the object of **Penal** or **Criminal Law**. The science of the fundamental concepts of Law has been called *Natural Law*, as if there were a law which belonged to man by nature and a different Law which originated in society in the sense that in this Law the Natural Law, as the true one, must to some extent be *sacrificed*. In fact society gives rise to particular laws which are not contained in the Law based on the individual personality. Society however, is at the same time the removal of the one-sidedness of the principle of the individual personality and its true realization.

Morality

189

Morality contains the proposition: In your action regard yourself as a free being; in other words it adds the moment of subjectivity to action, namely; (a) that the subjective element in the form of a Disposition and Intention shall correspond to what is in itself a commandment, and that what is a Duty shall be performed not from inclination or for the sake of some alien duty, or out of conceit of being good, but *because it is* **Duty**; (b) hence Morality concerns man as a particular individual and is not merely negative like Law. One can only let a free individual go his own way but to the particular individual something must be demonstrated.

190

The **Good** is the content of duties, namely, the fundamental determinations which contain the necessary human relationships or the rational element in them. **Evil** is what wilfully aims at the destruction of such relationships. The **Bad** is when duties are neglected, not with a direct intention, but knowingly, from weakness towards the sensuous impulse, or [by] an inclination of the heart.

191

(1) The necessary human relationship of each one to himself consists (a) in *self-preservation*, the individual subjecting external physical nature to himself and adjusting himself to it. (b) From his own Physical nature the individual must create the *independence* of his own Spiritual nature. (c) The individual must subject himself to, and make himself conformable to, his *Universal Spiritual Essence*: **Education**.

192

(2) The **Family Relationship** is the natural union of individuals. The bond of this natural society is love and trust, the knowledge of this original union and of action in accordance with it. According to their particular relationship the individuals composing this society possess particular rights; if these rights were asserted in the form of legal rights the moral bond of this society would be destroyed, that bond in which each receives what intrinsically belongs to him out of the sentiment of love.

193

(3) The moral relationship *to others generally* is based on the original

identity of human nature. The duties of the universal love of all men consist in a benevolent disposition and in the performance of general duties according to the accidental nature of the relationship. Moral obligations to closer and permanent performance of services arise from a relationship freely based on acquaintance and friendship.

The State (Real Spirit)

194

The natural society of the family expands into the universal society of the **State Society** [*Staatsgesellschaft*], which is just as much based on nature as it is on association freely entered into. It rests as much on Law as on Morality but, in general, appears essentially not as a society consisting of individuals as [rather] an inwardly united, individual **Spirit of the People**.

195

The **State Economy** [*Staatswissenschaft*] exhibits the *organization* possessed by People [*Volk*] as in itself a living organic Whole.

196

The State, as the universal, forms the antithesis to individuals. It is the more perfect the more the universal corresponds to reason and the more the individuals are one with the Spirit of the whole. The essential sentiment of the *citizens* [*Bürger*] towards the State is neither one of *blind obedience* to its commands, nor that each had to give his individual consent to its arrangements and regulations, but rather confidence in them and intelligent obedience.

197

The State contains various **Powers** which constitute the moments of its organization. The Legislative, Judicial and the Executive powers in general are its *abstract* moments. The *real* powers are those constituting the whole in each of which those abstract moments properly appear: the Judicial and Police, Financial and Administrative, Military and Political powers. The supreme activating centre of all is the **Government**.

198

The various **Estates** [*Stände*] of a State are in general concrete differences according to which individuals are divided into classes which rest principally on *inequality* of wealth, of connection and education [culture]. These again rest in part on inequality of birth whereby some individuals are more fitted for one activity in the service of the State than others.

199

The **Constitution** establishes the division and relation of the various State powers and the sphere of action of each, especially the rights of individuals in relation to the State and their share of participation in those powers which they ought to have, not merely in the choice of Government, but also in so far as they are simply citizens.

200

Customs, Laws and Constitution constitute the organized inner life of a national Spirit. The principle, or the kind and specific character of its essence, is expressed in them. In addition it has a relation to the outside world and external destinies.

201

This, so to speak, **Factual History** treats of the concrete existence of a people, the development of its principle in its constitution and laws and in its destinies, in an external fashion in accordance with perceived events and their immediate causes as they seem to lie in contingent circumstances and individual characters.

202

Philosophical History not only apprehends the principle of a nation from its institutions and destinies and develops the events from that principle, but considers especially the *universal World-Spirit*, how, in an inner context, through the history of nations in their separate appearances and their destinies, it has passed through the various stages of its formation. It exhibits the Universal Spirit in its accidents so that this shape or externality is not developed conformably to its essence. Its higher representation is its shaping in a simple spiritual form.

(Every nation does not count in world history. Each has its point, its moment, according to its principle. Then, as it seems, it departs for good. Its turn does not come by chance.)

THIRD SECTION
THE PURE EXHIBITION OF SPIRIT

Art

203

Art exhibits Spirit in individuality and, at the same time, purged of contingent existence and its changes and of external conditions, and that too *objectively* for intuition and representation. The **Beautiful** in its own essential nature is the object of Art, not the intuition of Nature which itself is only a temporal and unfree imitation of the Idea. **Aesthetics** treats of the more precise forms of this beautiful exhibition.

(Art depends on which substantial consciousness spirit is. We study the Greek works of art and are not therefore Greeks. It is not done by [mere] representation but by the inner productive life. The imaginative products of a people are not a superstitious belief in something but the nation's own Spirit; the so-called miraculous is a ridiculous bit of machinery; the angels and the Nordic gods of Klopstock are a misconception. It is the living mythology of a people, therefore, which constitutes the ground and substantial content of its Art.)

204

Two main forms of *styles* of art are to be distinguished, the **Antique** and the **Modern**. The character of the first is *plastic*, objective, that of the other, *romantic*, subjective. Antique art exhibits individuality at the same time as a universal, essential character without becoming on that account an abstraction and an allegory but remains a living totality. In its objective clarity and attitude it dissolves out the contingent and arbitrary element of subjectivity.

205

The **Arts** are distinguished by the *element* in which they portray the beautiful, whereby the object and spirit of this portrayal is more precisely defined. For *external* intuition *painting* gives a coloured shape on a surface, *sculpture* a colourless shape in bodily form. The *inner* intuition *music* employs the medium of unimaged sounds, *poetry* the medium of language.

(Oratory, architecture, the making of gardens, etc. are not pure fine arts, because they have another aim than to exhibit the beautiful.)

206

The chief kinds of **Poetry** are the *epic*, *lyric* and *dramatic*. The first depicts the object as an external event; the second, a single sentiment or a subjective movement in the heart; the third, action proper as an effect of the will.

Religion

207

Religion gives the exposition of Absolute Spirit not merely for intuition and pictorial thinking but also for thought and cognition. Its main function is to raise the individual to the thought of God, to bring him into union with God and to assure the individual of that union.

(Religion is the truth as it is for all men. The essence of true Religion is **Love**. It is essentially *disposition* as a knowledge of the truth of the human will. Religious Love is not merely a natural attachment or merely a moral benevolence: not a vague general feeble feeling; on the contrary it proves itself in the individual by an absolute sacrifice. 'Love one another as I have loved you.' (John XV, 12) Religious Love is the *infinite power* over all that is finite in Spirit, over what is bad, evil, criminal, even positive laws, etc. Christ allowed his disciples to pluck the ears of corn on the sabbath and healed a withered hand. Divine Love *forgives sins* and makes for Spirit what has happened as if it had never been. Much is forgiven Mary Magdalene because she loved much (Luke VII, 47). Love transcends even moral considerations: Mary anoints Christ instead of giving to the poor, and Christ approves this. The substantial relationship of man to God is the forgiveness of sins. The basis of Love is *the consciousness of God and his essential nature as Love* and Love therefore is the supreme humility. It is not I who am to be the objective element in Love but God; in knowing him I am to forget myself. The forgiveness of sins is not a temporal event, is not the consequence of an external punishment, but is an *external*, inner affair in the spirit and the heart. The nullifying of its nullity is the majesty of Love. The substantial relationship of man to God *seems* to be in its truth a *beyond*, but the love of God to man and of man to God overcomes the separation of the 'Here' and the 'Now' from what is represented as a Beyond and is *eternal life*.

This identity is *intuited in Christ*. As the Son of Man, he *is* the Son of God. For the God-man there is no beyond. He counts not as this *single* individual but as *universal* man, as true man. The external side of his history must be distinguished from the religious side. He has passed through the actual world, through lowliness, ignominy, has died. His *pain* was the depth of unity of the divine and the human nature in living suffering. The blessed gods of the heathens were represented as in a world beyond; through Christ, the ordinary actual world, this *lowliness* which is not contemptible, is *itself hallowed*. His resurrection and ascension are for faith alone: Stephen looked on his face and saw him standing on the right hand of God. God's eternal life is this, the return into himself. To let circumstantial details give rise to doubt as if this were an external reality is pitiful, childish. Faith is not at all concerned with sensuous history but with what eternally happens. **History of God**.

The *reconciliation* of God with man – as absolute happening, not as contingent, as a caprice of God – is known in the church. To know this is the Holy Spirit of the community. The **Kingdom of God** is primarily the *invisible church*, which embraces all regions and the various religions; then it is the church *in the world*. In the Roman Catholic church the community is divided within itself into priests and laity. The former possess authority and exercise power. Reconciliation with God is in part effected in external fashion; in general religion is a less spiritual reality among Roman Catholics. With Protestants, priests are only teachers. All in the community are equal before God as the present Spirit of the community. Works as such are powerless. It is faith, disposition, that is important. Evil is known as something absolutely null. This pain must pierce man. He must freely take hold of God's grace, uniting with him, in spite of evil, if he surrenders it and draws away from it. Only in the heart can there be an actual community with God. In the heart too the sensuous form of the sacraments is transfigured.)

Science

208

Science is the comprehensive knowledge of the Absolute Spirit. Since it is grasped in the *form* of the Concept, everything alien in knowledge is sublated and Knowing has attained to complete equality with itself. It is the Concept which has itself for content and comprehends itself.

BIBLIOGRAPHY

PRIMARY TEXTS UTILIZED

G. W. F. Hegel, *Werke*, vol. 18, ed. K. Rosenkranz, Berlin 1840.
G. W. F. Hegel, *Nürnberger Schriften*, ed. J. Hoffmeister, Leipzig 1938.
G. W. F. Hegel, *Nürnberger und Heidelberger Schriften 1808–1817*, *Werke*, vol. 4, ed. Eva Moldenhauer and Karl Markus Michel, Suhrkamp Verlag, Frankfurt-am-Main 1970.

HEGEL'S WORKS IN TRANSLATION

Early Theological Writings, trans. T. M. Knox, introduction by Richard Kroner, Chicago 1948.
Hegel's Political Writings, trans. T. M. Knox, introduction by Z. A. Pelczynski, Oxford 1964.
On the Difference between Fichte's and Schelling's System of Philosophy, trans. and ed. W. Cerf and H. S. Harris, Albany, N.Y. 1977.
The System of Ethical Life and First Philosophy of Spirit, trans. and ed. by H. S. Harris and T. M. Knox, Albany, N.Y. 1979.
Faith and Knowledge, trans. and ed. by W. Cerf and H. S. Harris, Albany, N.Y. 1977.
Natural Law, trans. T. M. Knox, introduction by H. B. Acton, Philadelphia, 1975
The Phenomenology of Spirit, trans. A. V. Miller, introduction by J. N. Findlay, Oxford 1977.
The Science of Logic, trans. A. V. Miller, London 1969.
The Philosophy of Right, trans. T. M. Knox, Oxford 1942.
Logic: Part One of the Encyclopaedia of the Philosophical Sciences, trans. W. Wallace, Oxford 1975.
Philosophy of Nature: Part Two of the Encyclopaedia of the Philosophical Sciences, trans. A. V. Miller, Oxford 1970.
Philosophy of Mind: Part Three of the Encyclopaedia of the Philosophical Sciences, trans. W. Wallace and A. V. Miller, Oxford 1971.

Lectures on the Philosophy of History, trans. J. Sibree, New York, N.Y. 1956. Also see *Lectures on the Philosophy of World History: Introduction: Reason in History*, trans. H. B. Nisbet, Cambridge 1975.
Lectures on the History of Philosophy, trans. E. S. Haldane and F. H. Simpson, in three volumes, London 1955.
Lectures on the Philosophy of Religion, trans. E. B. Spiers and J. B. Sanderson, in three volumes, London 1968.
Hegel's Aesthetics, trans. T. M. Knox, in two volumes, Oxford 1975.

SELECTED BIBLIOGRAPHY ON HEGEL'S PHILOSOPHY

Avineri, S. *Hegel's Theory of the Modern State*, Cambridge 1972.
Caird, E. *Hegel*, Edinburgh and London 1883.
Cullen, B. *Hegel's Social and Political Thought: An Introduction*, Dublin 1979.
Fackenheim, E. *The Religious Dimension in Hegel's Thought*, Bloomington, Ind. and London 1967.
Findlay, J. N. *Hegel: A Re-Examination*, London 1958.
Gadamer, H. G. *Hegel's Dialectic: Five Hermeneutical Studies*, trans. P. Christopher Smith, London 1976.
Harris, H. S. *Hegel's Development: Towards the Sunlight 1770–1801*, Oxford 1972.
—— *Hegel's Development: Night Thoughts (Jena 1801–06)*, Oxford 1983.
Hyppolite, J. *Genesis and Structure of Hegel's 'Phenomenology of Spirit'*, trans. S. Cherniak and J. Heckman, Evanston 1974.
Inwood, M. *Hegel*, Oxford 1983.
Kaufmann, W. *Hegel: Reinterpretation, Texts and Commentary*, London 1966.
—— *Hegel's Political Philosophy*, New York, N.Y. 1970.
Kelley, G. A. *Hegel's Retreat from Eleusis: Studies in Hegel's Political Thought*, Princeton, 1978.
Kojève, A. *Introduction to the Reading of Hegel: Lectures on the 'Phenomenology of Spirit'*, trans. J. H. Nichols, ed. by A. Bloom, New York, N.Y. 1969.
Lauer, Q. *A Reading of Hegel's 'Phenomenology of Spirit'*, New York, N.Y. 1976.
MacIntyre, A. (ed.) *Hegel: A Collection of Critical Essays*, New York, N.Y. 1972.
Mure, G. R. G. *The Philosophy of Hegel*, Oxford 1965.

Norman, R. *Hegel's Phenomenology: A Philosophical Introduction*, Brighton 1976.
Pelczynski, Z. A. (ed.) *Hegel's Political Philosophy: Problems and Perspectives*, Cambridge 1971.
—— (ed.) *The State and Civil Society: Studies in Hegel's Political Philosophy*, Cambridge 1984.
Plant, R. *Hegel*, London 1973, revised ed. Oxford 1983.
Reardon, B. *Hegel's Philosophy of Religion*, London 1977.
Reyburn, H. A. *The Ethical Theory of Hegel*, Oxford 1921.
Reidel, M. *Between Tradition and Revolution: The Hegelian Transformation of Political Philosophy*, Cambridge, Mass. 1982.
Rosen, S. *G. G. W. F. Hegel: An Introduction to the Science of Wisdom*, New Haven, Conn. 1974.
Shklar, J. N. *Freedom and Independence: A Study of the Political Ideas of Hegel's 'Phenomenology of Mind'*, Cambridge 1976.
Singer, P. *Hegel*, Oxford 1983.
Soll, I. *An Introduction to Hegel's Metaphysics*, Chicago, Ill. 1969.
Solomon, R. *In the Spirit of Hegel: A Study of Hegel's Phenomenology*, Oxford 1983.
Steinkraus, W. E. (ed.) *New Studies in the Philosophy of Hegel*, New York, N.Y. 1971.
Steinkraus, W. E. and Schmitz, K. L. (eds) *Art and Logic in Hegel's Philosophy*, New Jersey and Brighton 1980.
Stepelevitch, L. S. and Lamb, D. (eds) *Hegel's Philosophy of Action*, Brighton 1983.
Taylor, C. *Hegel*, Cambridge 1975.
—— *Hegel and Modern Society*, Cambridge 1979.
Toews, J. E. *Hegelianism: The Path Towards Dialectical Humanism*, Cambridge 1980.
Verene, D. P. (ed.) *Hegel's Social and Political Thought: the Philosophy of Objective Spirit*, New Jersey, Pa. and Brighton 1980.
Walsh, W. H. *Hegelian Ethics*, London 1969.
Westphal, M. *History and Truth in Hegel's 'Phenomenology'*, New Jersey, Pa. and Brighton 1979.
Wiedman, F. *Hegel: An Illustrated Biography*, New York, N.Y. 1968.

INDEX

abstract object, 4
  idea, 4
  representation, 4
  will, 22
abstraction, 4, 75
act, 2, 3, 10–11, 15
actuality, 87–90, 133
aesthetics, xix, 167
antinomies, xviii, 90–6
appearance, 83–6
  and content, 85
  and form, 84
  and inner and outer, 86
  and matter, 84
  and mutual relation, 84
  and things and properties, 83
  and wholes and parts, 83
appetite
  higher, 2, 11
  lower, 2
arbitrariness, 3, 17
art, 167–8
attention, 8
authority, 5

being, 76–7, 127
  determinate, xxvii–xxviii, 77–8, 127–8
  nothing and becoming, xxvi, 77, 127
Bildung, xx
blessedness, 21

categories, 67
causality, 9
cause, 133

chemical sphere, 118
citizen, xxi
classics, xv–xvii
cognition of the good, 120–2
concept, 6, 76, 105–17, 134
  doctrine of, 67
  and reality, 104
  realization of, 117–19
consciousness, xviii, 56–9
  perceiving, 57
  practical, 2, 7–8
  and reason, 63–4
  and self-consciousness, 59–63
  sensuous, 57
  theoretical, 1, 7–8
  and understanding, 57
constitutions, 34–5, 166
contract, 28
curriculum, xiv, xxi

deed, 15
desire, 59, 60
discipline, xiv
disposition, 20, 37
dreams, 154
duties, 41–52

education, xiii–xxi, 18, 164
  practical, 43–4
  theoretic, 42–3
encyclopaedia, xviii, 124–5
end, 103, 117, 139–40
essence, 81–3, 130–2
estates, 166–7
evil, 50, 53, 164
experience, 5

family, 32, 46, 164
fate, 44
feeling, 6, 150, 161
finitude, 13
fortune, 21
freedom, xxi, 14, 17–9
  abstract, 3
  political, 14–5
  see also will
friendship, 51

good, 6, 50, 164
government, 33, 165
ground, 131–2

happiness, 38
history, 166

Idea, 76, 104, 127, 140–2
Idealism, 55
imagination, 8, 153
impulse, 2, 11, 40, 60
instinct, 11
intuition, 9, 151

Judgement, 24, 68–73, 99–103, 107–17, 134–6
  apodictic, 72, 102, 113
  assertoric, 71, 101, 102, 112
  categorical, 71, 101, 111, 135
  and copula, 68, 107
  disjunctive, 71, 101, 112, 135
  hypothetical, 71, 101, 112, 135
  identical, 109
  individual, 70
  infinite, 70, 101, 109, 135
  modality of, 102–3, 112
  negative, 69, 100, 108, 109, 135
  particular, 70, 101, 135
  positive, 69, 100, 108, 135
  and predicate, 68, 107
  problematic, 102, 112
  and proposition, 107
  qualitative, 69, 100, 108, 135
  of reflection, 110
  of relation, 101
  singular, 135
  and subject, 68, 107
  universal, 101, 135

knowing, 55, 122–3, 142

language, 8, 157–8
law, 19, 22–31, 33, 35–6, 162, 163
life, 104, 119–20, 140–2
logic, xviii, xxii–xxiii, 65–123, 125
  formal, 97
  objective, 76, 105–23
  ontological, 127–33
  subjective, 76, 96, 127, 134–40
love, 168

marriage, 46
master–slave, 59–63
mathematics, 143–5
measure, 80–1
mechanism, 118
mediation, 118
memory, 156–7
moral action, 37, 40–1
moral will, 21
morality and law, 19, 164

nature, xviii–xix, xxiii, 125, 143–9
  see also logic; spirit

object, 4
obligation, 36, 41–52
organic nature, 147–9

particularity, 67, 98
patriotism, 47
people, spirit of, 47
perception, 4, 5, 57
person, 23
phenomenology, xviii, 55–64
physics, 145–47
pleasure, 21, 38–9
political society, 32
possession, 24, 162
powers (of the state), 34
practical spirit, 160–6

properties (and accidents), 58
property, 24–8, 162–3
proposition, 107, 130–1
prudence, 44, 51
psychology, xviii, 56
punishment, 31, 163

quality, 78, 127–8
quantity, 79–80, 128–9
quantum, 129

realism, 55
reason, 39–40, 56, 63–4, 159–60
  and truth, 64
  and the understanding, 58
reciprocity, 133
recollection, 151, 152
reflection, 2, 12, 13, 39
religion, 21, 52–4, 168–9
representation, 65–6, 75, 150–1
right (lawful), 6

science
  and absolute idea, 104, 169
  of the concept, 105–17
  and the idea, 119–23
  and philosophy, xix
  and realization, 117–23
self-consciousness, 59–63
sensation, 65

space and time, 66, 143
speech, 8
spirit, xx–xxi, xxiii–xxiv, 125, 149–67
  see also logic; nature
state, 32, 47–52, 165
  of nature, 33
syllogism, 72–3, 102–3, 113–17, 136–8

teleological concept, 103
temperance, 43
thing, 57, 83
thought (thinking), 8–10, 65–6, 74–5, 158–60
truth, 64, 77, 108, 122–3

understanding, 58, 126
universal, 67, 105, 134

virtue, 45

will, xxviii–xxx, 16–8, 23, 24
  abstract, 22
  of choice, 3, 17
  and freedom, 14–15, 16, 18
  particular, 1
  pure, 4, 18
  universal, 1, 16, 22
world, 1
writing, 8